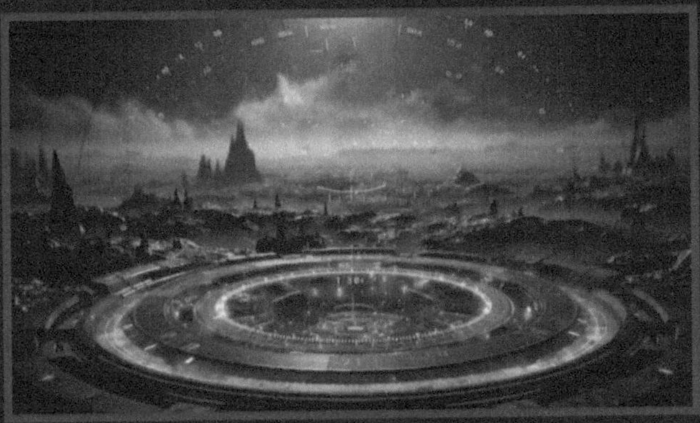

RESTful API Development with Django

With real-world examples, practical exercises, and insightful tips, Transform Data into Powerful Application. Build Scalable APIs and Rule the Digital World and more !

Katie Millie

RESTful API Development with Django

With real-world examples, practical exercises, and insightful tips, Transform Data into Powerful Application. Build Scalable APIs and Rule the Digital World and more !

By

Katie Millie

Copyright notice

Copyright © 2024 Katie Millie. All rights reserved.

Unauthorized reproduction, distribution, or transmission of any content from this website, whether through photocopying, recording, or any electronic or mechanical means, is strictly prohibited without prior written consent from Katie Millie. The only exceptions to this rule are for brief quotations used in critical reviews or other noncommercial purposes permitted by copyright law.

Please note that all product names, logos, and brands mentioned on this website belong to their respective owners. Their inclusion here is solely for identification purposes and does not constitute endorsement by Katie Millie.

While every effort has been taken to ensure the accuracy and currency of the information provided on this website, Katie Millie cannot be held responsible for any inaccuracies or damages that may arise from its use.

Users are encouraged to verify any critical information before relying on it.

Table of Contents

INTRODUCTION

Chapter 1

    Understanding the Power of APIs and Data Exchange

        Demystifying RESTful APIs: The Universal Language of Applications

            Unveiling the Benefits of Building RESTful APIs with Django

Chapter 2

    Introduction to Django: Building Web Applications and APIs with Python

        Essential Django Concepts: Models, Views, and URLs

            Setting Up Your Django Development Environment: Let's Get Coding!

Chapter 3

    Demystifying REST: Core Principles for Building Powerful APIs

        HTTP Methods in RESTful APIs: GET, POST, PUT, DELETE, and Beyond

            Designing a Clear and Consistent API Structure

Chapter 4

    Designing Robust Data Models for Your API using Django Models

        Defining Relationships Between Models: Building Complex Data Structures

            Serializers: Transforming Data into

Consumable API Formats

Chapter 5

Understanding Django's URL Routing System for APIs

Defining Resource Endpoints: Mapping URLs to API Functionality

Building RESTful URLs: Aligning with RESTful Design Principles

Chapter 6

Crafting Views in Django for Handling API Requests

Processing Data and Performing Operations within Views

Building RESTful Views: Implementing GET, POST, PUT, and DELETE Methods

Chapter 7

Guarding Your Fortress: Authentication and Authorization in APIs

Defining User Permissions and Authorization Levels in Django RESTful APIs

Protecting Your API from Unauthorized Access and Vulnerabilities

Chapter 8

Introduction to API Testing: Guaranteeing Functionality and Reliability

Unit Testing, Integration Testing, and End-to-End Testing for APIs

Utilizing Testing Frameworks for Streamlined Testing Processes

Chapter 9

Understanding the Need for API Versioning

Implementing Versioning Strategies to Maintain

Compatibility
  Handling Versioning Requests and Maintaining API Stability

Chapter 10
  The Importance of Clear and Concise API Documentation
    Utilizing Tools and Standards for Effective API Documentation
      Enabling Developers to Easily Understand and Utilize Your API

Chapter 12
  Optimizing Performance for Scalability and High Traffic Volumes
    Caching Strategies, Database Optimization, and Efficient Code Practices
      Ensuring Your API Remains Responsive and Efficient
        Choosing the Right Hosting Platform for Your Production API
          Configuring Your Django Application for Deployment

Chapter 13
  Django REST Framework: Building RESTful APIs with Streamlined Functionality
    Integrating with Other Systems: Utilizing Django APIs in Different Applications
      Building Scalable and Secure API Ecosystems

Conclusion
  Appendix
    Common Django Libraries and Tools for API

Development
    Troubleshooting Tips and Error Handling in
    Django APIs
        Glossary of terms

INTRODUCTION

Forge Your Digital Empire: RESTful API Development with Django

Imagine a world where your data becomes the fuel that powers innovative applications. A world where your meticulously crafted backend effortlessly connects with mobile apps, web interfaces, and beyond. This, my friend, is the power of RESTful APIs, and Django, the Python web framework giant, is your key to unlocking it.

RESTful API Development with Django isn't just another technical manual; it's your personal roadmap to becoming an API architect extraordinaire. Forget confusing jargon and overwhelming complexity – here, we break down the art of building robust, scalable APIs using Django's intuitive features and clear structure.

Why RESTful APIs and Django?

RESTful APIs, with their standardized approach, are the lingua franca of the modern web. They allow seamless communication between different applications, fostering a world of interconnectedness and boundless possibilities.Django, the Python champion, empowers you to build these APIs efficiently, leveraging its built-in tools and functionalities to streamline the development process.

But here's the real magic – with Django, you're not just limited to APIs. You get the best of both worlds: a framework that excels at crafting beautiful web applications and APIs that act as the invisible backbone connecting everything.

Unveiling the Secrets of API Architects

This book is your comprehensive guide, taking you step-by-step from the fundamentals to crafting production-ready APIs. Here's a glimpse of the exciting journey that awaits:

- **Demystifying REST:** We'll delve into the core principles of RESTful APIs, ensuring you understand the underlying concepts that make them powerful and versatile.
- **Django's API Arsenal:** Explore Django's built-in functionalities like models, views, and serializers – the essential tools that transform your data into a consumable API format.
- **URL Routing Mastery:** Craft intuitive and well-structured URLs that act as the entry points for your API, allowing applications to access data effortlessly.
- **Authentication and Authorization:** Learn how to safeguard your API with robust authentication mechanisms, ensuring only authorized users access your valuable data.
- **Testing Your Masterpiece:** Master the art of testing your API, guaranteeing its reliability and functionality before unleashing it to the world.

Beyond the Basics: Power Up Your APIs

This book goes far beyond the rudimentary aspects of building APIs. We'll equip you with advanced techniques to elevate your skills:

- **Versioning Your API:** Learn how to gracefully handle API versioning, ensuring a smooth transition even as your API evolves.
- **Documentation for Developers:** Craft clear and concise documentation so other developers can easily understand and utilize your API.
- **Performance Optimization:** Dive into performance optimization strategies to ensure your API remains fast and scalable even under heavy traffic.
- **Deployment Strategies:** We'll guide you through the process of deploying your API to a production environment, making it accessible to the world.

RESTful API Development with Django isn't just about technical prowess; it's about empowering you to become a confident and creative API architect. We'll provide real-world examples, practical exercises, and insightful tips to ignite your passion for building APIs that solve real-world problems.

This book is your launchpad to a world of possibilities, where your data becomes the foundation for limitless innovation. So, are you ready to forge your digital empire? Grab your copy today and start building APIs that power the future!

Chapter 1

Understanding the Power of APIs and Data Exchange

In today's interconnected digital landscape, the power of APIs (Application Programming Interfaces) and data exchange cannot be overstated. APIs serve as the backbone of modern software development, enabling different applications to communicate with each other and exchange data seamlessly. In this discourse, we'll delve into the significance of APIs, their role in data exchange, and how to develop RESTful APIs using Django, a high-level Python web framework.

What are APIs?

APIs are sets of rules and protocols that allow different software applications to communicate with each other. They define the methods and data formats that applications can use to request and exchange information. APIs abstract away the complexities of underlying systems, enabling developers to leverage functionalities provided by other applications without needing to understand their internal workings.

The Importance of APIs

1. Interoperability: APIs facilitate interoperability between diverse systems and platforms, allowing them to work together seamlessly. This interoperability is crucial for building integrated ecosystems where different applications complement each other's functionalities.

2. Flexibility: APIs enable developers to build modular, flexible systems by breaking down complex functionalities into smaller, manageable components. This modularity promotes code reuse, simplifies maintenance, and accelerates development.

3. Scalability: By exposing specific functionalities via APIs, applications can scale more efficiently to accommodate growing user demands. APIs abstract away the underlying infrastructure complexities, allowing applications to scale horizontally or vertically without disrupting the overall system architecture.

4. Innovation: APIs foster innovation by enabling developers to combine and remix functionalities from different applications to create new and innovative solutions. They empower developers to experiment, iterate, and build upon existing technologies, driving continuous innovation across various domains.

Understanding RESTful APIs

REST (Representational State Transfer) is an architectural style for designing networked applications. RESTful APIs adhere to the principles of REST, making them simple, scalable, and easy to understand. They leverage HTTP methods (GET, POST, PUT, DELETE) to perform CRUD (Create, Read, Update, Delete) operations on resources, making them ideal for building web services and APIs.

Developing RESTful APIs with Django

Django is a powerful web framework for building web applications in Python. It provides built-in support for developing RESTful APIs using its Django REST Framework (DRF) library. Let's explore the key steps involved in developing RESTful APIs with Django:

1. Setting up a Django Project: Begin by installing Django and creating a new Django project using the `django-admin` command-line utility. Once the project is set up, create a new Django app within the project to house your API code.

2. Defining Models: Define your data models using Django's Object-Relational Mapping (ORM) system. Models represent the structure of your data and are essential for interacting with the database. Define models for the resources you intend to expose via your API.

3. Serializers: Serializers in Django REST Framework translate complex data types (e.g., model instances) into native Python data types (e.g., JSON) that can be easily rendered into HTTP responses. Create serializers for your models to specify how data should be serialized and deserialized.

4. Views: Views in Django REST Framework are similar to Django views but tailored for API endpoints. Define views for your API endpoints, specifying the logic for handling various HTTP methods (GET, POST, PUT, DELETE) on each endpoint.

5. URL Routing: Define URL patterns to map incoming HTTP requests to the appropriate views. Use Django's URL routing system to define patterns for your API endpoints, making them accessible via unique URLs.

6. Authentication and Permissions: Implement authentication and permissions to secure your API endpoints. Django REST Framework provides built-in support for various authentication mechanisms (e.g., token authentication, session authentication) and permissions (e.g., IsAuthenticated, IsAdminUser).

7. Testing: Write comprehensive unit tests to ensure the correctness and robustness of your API endpoints. Django provides tools for writing and running tests, allowing you to automate the testing process and catch potential issues early.

8. Documentation: Document your API endpoints to help developers understand how to use them effectively. Use tools like Django REST Swagger or Django REST Framework's built-in documentation generator to generate interactive API documentation from your code.

By following these steps, you can develop powerful RESTful APIs with Django that facilitate seamless data exchange between different applications and systems. APIs empower developers to build innovative solutions, drive interoperability, and unlock the full potential of modern software development. Embrace the power of APIs and data exchange to create interconnected digital ecosystems that drive innovation and accelerate progress.

Demystifying RESTful APIs: The Universal Language of Applications

In the ever-evolving landscape of software development, RESTful APIs have emerged as the universal language that allows applications to communicate and interact seamlessly. RESTful APIs provide a standardized approach for building web services, enabling different systems to exchange data and functionalities over the internet. In this discourse, we'll delve into the fundamentals of RESTful APIs, their significance in modern application development, and how to develop them using Django, a high-level Python web framework.

Understanding RESTful APIs

REST, which stands for Representational State Transfer, is an architectural style for designing networked applications. RESTful APIs adhere to the principles of REST, making them simple, scalable, and easy to understand. At the core of RESTful APIs are resources, which represent entities or objects that the API exposes. These resources are manipulated using standard HTTP methods, such as GET, POST, PUT, and DELETE, corresponding to CRUD (Create, Read, Update, Delete) operations.

The key principles of RESTful APIs include:

1. Statelessness: RESTful APIs are stateless, meaning that each request from a client to the server contains all the information necessary for the server to understand and fulfill the request. This simplifies server implementation and improves scalability.

2. Uniform Interface: RESTful APIs have a uniform interface, which means that they adhere to a standardized set of conventions for interacting with resources. This includes using HTTP methods to perform operations on resources and following a consistent URI structure for resource identification.

3. Client-Server Architecture: RESTful APIs follow a client-server architecture, where clients and servers are separate entities that communicate over the network. This separation of concerns allows for more scalable and modular systems.

4. Resource-Based: RESTful APIs are resource-based, meaning that they model resources as the primary abstraction. Resources are identified by unique URIs (Uniform Resource Identifiers) and can be represented in different formats, such as JSON or XML.

The Significance of RESTful APIs

RESTful APIs play a pivotal role in modern application development for several reasons:

1. Interoperability: RESTful APIs facilitate interoperability between diverse systems and platforms. By adhering to standardized conventions and protocols,

RESTful APIs enable different applications to communicate and exchange data seamlessly, regardless of their underlying technologies.

2. Scalability: RESTful APIs are inherently scalable, allowing applications to handle increasing volumes of traffic and users. Because they are stateless and use standard HTTP protocols, RESTful APIs can be deployed across distributed environments and scaled horizontally to meet growing demands.

3. Flexibility: RESTful APIs provide a flexible and modular architecture, allowing developers to design APIs that cater to specific use cases and requirements. They promote code reusability, simplifying the development and maintenance of complex systems.

4. Ecosystem Integration: RESTful APIs enable the integration of disparate systems and services into cohesive ecosystems. By exposing functionalities as APIs, organizations can leverage existing investments in technology and infrastructure, fostering innovation and collaboration across domains.

Developing RESTful APIs with Django

Django is a popular web framework for building web applications in Python. It provides robust tools and libraries for developing RESTful APIs through its Django REST Framework (DRF) extension. Let's explore the key steps involved in developing RESTful APIs with Django:

1. Setting up a Django Project: Begin by installing Django and creating a new Django project using the `django-admin` command-line utility. Once the project is set up, create a new Django app within the project to house your API code.

```bash
pip install django
django-admin startproject myproject
cd myproject
django-admin startapp myapp
```

2. Defining Models: Define your data models using Django's Object-Relational Mapping (ORM) system. Models represent the structure of your data and are essential for interacting with the database. Define models for the resources you intend to expose via your API.

```python
# models.py

from django.db import models
```

```python
class Product(models.Model):
    name = models.CharField(max_length=100)
    price = models.DecimalField(max_digits=10, decimal_places=2)
    description = models.TextField()
```

3. Serializers: Serializers in Django REST Framework translate complex data types (e.g., model instances) into native Python data types (e.g., JSON) that can be easily rendered into HTTP responses. Create serializers for your models to specify how data should be serialized and deserialized.

```python
# serializers.py

from rest_framework import serializers
from .models import Product

class ProductSerializer(serializers.ModelSerializer):
    class Meta:
        model = Product
        fields = ['id', 'name', 'price', 'description']
```

4. Views: Views in Django REST Framework are similar to Django views but tailored for API endpoints. Define views for your API endpoints, specifying the logic for handling various HTTP methods (GET, POST, PUT, DELETE) on each endpoint.

```python
views.py

from rest_framework import generics
from .models import Product
from .serializers import ProductSerializer

class ProductList(generics.ListCreateAPIView):
    queryset = Product.objects.all()
    serializer_class = ProductSerializer

class ProductDetail(generics.RetrieveUpdateDestroyAPIView):
    queryset = Product.objects.all()
    serializer_class = ProductSerializer
```

5. URL Routing: Define URL patterns to map incoming HTTP requests to the appropriate views. Use Django's URL routing system to define patterns for your API endpoints, making them accessible via unique URLs.

```python
# urls.py

from django.urls import path
from .views import ProductList, ProductDetail

urlpatterns = [
    path('products/', ProductList.as_view(), name='product-list'),
    path('products/<int:pk>/', ProductDetail.as_view(), name='product-detail'),
```

6. **Authentication and Permissions:** Implement authentication and permissions to secure your API endpoints. Django REST Framework provides built-in support for various authentication mechanisms (e.g., token authentication, session authentication) and permissions (e.g., IsAuthenticated, IsAdminUser).

```python
# settings.py

REST_FRAMEWORK = {
    'DEFAULT_AUTHENTICATION_CLASSES': [

'rest_framework.authentication.TokenAuthentication',
```

```
    'rest_framework.authentication.SessionAuthentication',
    ],
    'DEFAULT_PERMISSION_CLASSES': [
        'rest_framework.permissions.IsAuthenticated',
}
```

7. Testing: Write comprehensive unit tests to ensure the correctness and robustness of your API endpoints. Django provides tools for writing and running tests, allowing you to automate the testing process and catch potential issues early.

```python
# tests.py

from django.test import TestCase
from django.urls import reverse
from rest_framework import status
from rest_framework.test import APIClient
from .models import Product

class ProductTests(TestCase):
    def setUp(self):
        self.client = APIClient()
        self.product = Product.objects.create(name='Test Product', price=10.00, description='Test Description')
```

```python
    def test_get_products(self):
        url = reverse('product-list')
        response = self.client.get(url)
        self.assertEqual(response.status_code, status.HTTP_200_OK)
        self.assertEqual(len(response.data), 1)

    def test_create_product(self):
        url = reverse('product-list')
        data = {'name': 'New Product', 'price': 20.00, 'description': 'New Description'}
        response = self.client.post(url, data)
        self.assertEqual(response.status_code, status.HTTP_201_CREATED)

    def test_update_product(self):
        url = reverse('product-detail', args=[self.product.id])
        data = {'name': 'Updated Product', 'price': 30.00, 'description': 'Updated Description'}
        response = self.client.put(url, data)
        self.assertEqual(response.status_code, status.HTTP_200_OK)
        self.product.refresh_from_db()
        self.assertEqual(self.product.name, 'Updated Product')

    def test_delete_product(self):
```

```
        url = reverse('product-detail', args=[self.product.id])
        response = self.client.delete(url)
        self.assertEqual(response.status_code, status.HTTP_204_NO_CONTENT)

self.assertFalse(Product.objects.filter(id=self.product.id).exists())
```

8. Documentation: Document your API endpoints to help developers understand how to use them effectively. Use tools like Django REST Swagger or Django REST Framework's built-in documentation generator to generate interactive API documentation from your code.

```python
# urls.py

from django.urls import path, include
from rest_framework.documentation import include_docs_urls

urlpatterns = [
    path('docs/', include_docs_urls(title='My API Documentation')),
    # Other API URL patterns
]
```

By following these steps, you can develop robust and scalable RESTful APIs with Django. These APIs serve as the universal language that enables applications to communicate and exchange data effortlessly. Embrace the power of RESTful APIs to build interconnected systems, foster innovation, and drive the next wave of digital transformation.

Unveiling the Benefits of Building RESTful APIs with Django

In the realm of web development, the adoption of RESTful APIs has become ubiquitous due to their ability to facilitate seamless communication and data exchange between applications. When it comes to developing RESTful APIs, Django, a high-level Python web framework, stands out as a powerful tool for building robust and scalable APIs. In this discourse, we'll explore the myriad benefits of building RESTful APIs with Django, along with practical examples and code snippets to illustrate key concepts.

1. Rapid Development

Django's philosophy of "batteries-included" means that it comes with a plethora of built-in features and tools that streamline the development process. When building

RESTful APIs with Django, developers can leverage these features to expedite development and focus on implementing business logic rather than reinventing the wheel.

Example:

```python
# models.py

from django.db import models

class Product(models.Model):
    name = models.CharField(max_length=100)
    price = models.DecimalField(max_digits=10, decimal_places=2)
    description = models.TextField()
```

2. Django REST Framework (DRF)

Django REST Framework (DRF) is a powerful extension of Django that provides additional tools and utilities specifically designed for building RESTful APIs. DRF simplifies common tasks such as serialization, authentication, and URL routing, allowing developers to build APIs with minimal boilerplate code.

Example:

```python
# serializers.py

from rest_framework import serializers
from .models import Product

class ProductSerializer(serializers.ModelSerializer):
    class Meta:
        model = Product
        fields = ['id', 'name', 'price', 'description']
```

3. Scalability

Scalability is a critical aspect of any application, especially when it comes to handling large volumes of traffic and users. Django's architecture, combined with the stateless nature of RESTful APIs, enables applications to scale horizontally by adding more servers or instances to distribute the workload.

Example:

```python
# settings.py
```

ALLOWED_HOSTS = ['*'] # Allow requests from any host for scalability
```

## 4. Authentication and Permissions

Django provides robust authentication and permission systems out of the box, which can be seamlessly integrated into RESTful APIs. Whether you need token-based authentication, session authentication, or custom authentication schemes, Django's authentication framework has you covered.

**Example**:

```python
# settings.py

REST_FRAMEWORK = {
    'DEFAULT_AUTHENTICATION_CLASSES': [

'rest_framework.authentication.TokenAuthentication',

'rest_framework.authentication.SessionAuthentication',
    ],
    'DEFAULT_PERMISSION_CLASSES': [
        'rest_framework.permissions.IsAuthenticated',
}

```

5. Comprehensive Documentation

Documenting APIs is crucial for ensuring that developers understand how to use them effectively. Django REST Framework provides built-in tools for generating interactive API documentation from your code, making it easy to create comprehensive and user-friendly documentation for your APIs.

Example:

```python
# urls.py

from django.urls import path, include
from rest_framework.documentation import include_docs_urls

urlpatterns = [
    path('docs/', include_docs_urls(title='My API Documentation')),
    # Other API URL patterns
]
```

6. Testing and Debugging
```

Django encourages best practices such as test-driven development (TDD), making it easy to write comprehensive unit tests for your RESTful APIs. Django's testing framework provides tools for writing and running tests, allowing you to catch bugs early and ensure the correctness of your APIs.

Example:

```python
# tests.py

from django.test import TestCase
from django.urls import reverse
from rest_framework import status
from rest_framework.test import APIClient
from .models import Product

class ProductTests(TestCase):
    def setUp(self):
        self.client = APIClient()
        self.product = Product.objects.create(name='Test Product', price=10.00, description='Test Description')

    def test_get_products(self):
        url = reverse('product-list')
        response = self.client.get(url)
```

```
        self.assertEqual(response.status_code, status.HTTP_200_OK)
        self.assertEqual(len(response.data), 1)
```

7. Community and Ecosystem

Django boasts a vibrant and active community of developers who contribute plugins, extensions, and resources to the ecosystem. Whether you need authentication libraries, third-party integrations, or advanced features, chances are there's a Django package available to meet your needs.

Example:

```python
# requirements.txt

django
djangorestframework
```

Building RESTful APIs with Django offers numerous benefits, ranging from rapid development and scalability to comprehensive documentation and testing capabilities. By leveraging Django's robust features and the Django REST Framework, developers can build APIs that are efficient, secure, and easy to maintain. As the demand for interconnected systems continues to grow, Django remains a top choice for building RESTful APIs that power the modern web.

Chapter 2

Introduction to Django: Building Web Applications and APIs with Python

Django, a high-level Python web framework, has gained widespread popularity for its simplicity, scalability, and versatility in building web applications and APIs. With its "batteries-included" approach, Django provides developers with a robust set of tools and libraries to streamline the development process and build secure and maintainable applications. In this introduction, we'll explore the fundamentals of Django, its core components, and how to leverage it to build web applications and APIs, with a focus on RESTful API development.

What is Django?

Django is a powerful web framework written in Python that follows the Model-View-Controller (MVC) architectural pattern, although it refers to it as Model-View-Template (MVT). Django's primary goal is to enable developers to build web applications quickly and efficiently by providing a structured and pragmatic approach to web development. Django emphasizes reusability, modularity, and the principle of "don't repeat yourself" (DRY), which helps developers write clean and maintainable code.

Key Features of Django:

1. Object-Relational Mapping (ORM): Django's ORM allows developers to interact with the database using high-level Python objects, eliminating the need to write raw SQL queries. This abstraction simplifies database operations and promotes code reusability.

2. Admin Interface: Django provides a built-in admin interface that allows developers to manage application data through a web-based administrative interface. The admin interface is highly customizable and can be tailored to fit the specific requirements of the application.

3. URL Routing: Django's URL routing system allows developers to define URL patterns that map to views, enabling clean and readable URL structures. URL routing is essential for building RESTful APIs and organizing the application's URLs logically.

4. Template Engine: Django's template engine enables developers to build dynamic web pages using HTML templates with embedded Python code. Templates facilitate code reuse and separation of concerns by separating the presentation layer from the business logic.

5. Security Features: Django comes with built-in security features, including protection against common web vulnerabilities such as cross-site scripting (XSS), cross-site request forgery (CSRF), and SQL injection. Django's security features help developers build secure web applications by default.

6. Middleware: Django middleware provides a mechanism for processing HTTP requests and responses in a customizable and reusable way. Middleware can perform tasks such as authentication, logging, and content compression, enhancing the application's functionality and performance.

7. Internationalization and Localization: Django supports internationalization (i18n) and localization (l10n) out of the box, allowing developers to build applications that support multiple languages and cultural conventions. Django's internationalization features make it easy to translate application content into different languages.

Building Web Applications with Django:

To illustrate how Django works, let's walk through the process of building a simple web application for managing products. We'll cover the following steps:

1. Setting up a Django Project: Begin by installing Django and creating a new Django project using the `django-admin` command-line utility.

```bash

pip install django

django-admin startproject myproject

cd myproject
```

```

**2. Creating a Django App:** Within the Django project, create a new Django app to house your application's code.

```bash
django-admin startapp myapp
```

3. Defining Models: Define your data models using Django's ORM system. Models represent the structure of your application's data and are essential for interacting with the database.

```python
# models.py

from django.db import models

class Product(models.Model):
    name = models.CharField(max_length=100)
    price = models.DecimalField(max_digits=10, decimal_places=2)
    description = models.TextField()
```
```

4. Admin Interface: Register your models with the Django admin interface to enable CRUD operations on your application's data.

```python
# admin.py

from django.contrib import admin

from .models import Product

admin.site.register(Product)
```

5. URL Routing: Define URL patterns to map incoming HTTP requests to views within your application.

```python
# urls.py

from django.urls import path

from . import views

urlpatterns = [

    path('products/', views.ProductListView.as_view(), name='product-list'),
```

```
    path('products/<int:pk>/',
views.ProductDetailView.as_view(), name='product-detail'),
```

6. Views: Define views to handle HTTP requests and generate responses. Views encapsulate the business logic of your application.

```python
# views.py

from django.shortcuts import render

from django.views.generic import ListView, DetailView

from .models import Product

class ProductListView(ListView):

    model = Product

    template_name = 'product_list.html'

class ProductDetailView(DetailView):

    model = Product

    template_name = 'product_detail.html'
```

7. Templates: Create HTML templates to render the user interface of your application. Templates allow you to define the structure and layout of web pages.

```html
<!-- product_list.html -->
<!DOCTYPE html>
<html lang="en">
<head>
    <meta charset="UTF-8">
    <title>Product List</title>
</head>
<body>
    <h1>Product List</h1>
    <ul>
        {% for product in object_list %}
            <li><a href="{% url 'product-detail' product.pk %}">{{ product.name }}</a></li>
        {% endfor %}
    </ul>
```

```
</body>

</html>
```

8. Running the Development Server: Finally, start the Django development server to run your application locally and test it in a web browser.

```bash
python manage.py runserver
```

By following these steps, you can build a simple web application with Django that allows users to view a list of products and navigate to individual product details. Django's built-in features and conventions make it easy to develop web applications quickly and efficiently, making it an ideal choice for building a wide range of web applications.

Building RESTful APIs with Django:

In addition to building traditional web applications, Django is also well-suited for building RESTful APIs that expose data and functionality over the internet. To build RESTful APIs with Django, developers can leverage the Django REST Framework (DRF), an extension of Django that provides additional tools and utilities for building APIs. Let's walk through the process of building a simple RESTful API for managing products using Django and DRF:

1. Installing Django REST Framework:

```bash
pip install djangorestframework
```

2. Serializers: Define serializers to convert Django model instances into JSON representations that can be rendered into HTTP responses.

```python
# serializers.py

from rest_framework import serializers

from .models import Product

class ProductSerializer(serializers.ModelSerializer):
    class Meta:
        model = Product
        fields = ['id', 'name', 'price', 'description']
```

3. Views: Define views using DRF's view classes to handle HTTP requests and generate responses for API endpoints.

```python
# views.py

from rest_framework import generics

from .models import Product

from .serializers import ProductSerializer

class ProductListCreate(generics.ListCreateAPIView):

    queryset = Product.objects.all()

    serializer_class = ProductSerializer

class ProductRetrieveUpdateDestroy(generics.RetrieveUpdateDestroyAPIView):

    queryset = Product.objects.all()

    serializer_class = ProductSerializer
```

4. URL Routing: Define URL patterns to map incoming HTTP requests to DRF views within your application.

```python
```

```python
# urls.py

from django.urls import path

from . import views

urlpatterns = [

    path('api/products/', views.ProductListCreate.as_view(), name='product-list-create'),

    path('api/products/<int:pk>/', views.ProductRetrieveUpdateDestroy.as_view(), name='product-retrieve-update-destroy'),

]
```

5. Authentication and Permissions: Implement authentication and permissions to secure your API endpoints. DRF provides built-in support for various authentication mechanisms and permissions.

```python
# settings.py

REST_FRAMEWORK = {

    'DEFAULT_AUTHENTICATION_CLASSES': [
```

```
'rest_framework.authentication.TokenAuthentication',

'rest_framework.authentication.SessionAuthentication',
    ],
    'DEFAULT_PERMISSION_CLASSES': [
        'rest_framework.permissions.IsAuthenticated',
```

6. Testing: Write comprehensive unit tests to ensure the correctness and robustness of your API endpoints.

```python
# tests.py
from django.test import TestCase
from django.urls import reverse
from rest_framework import status
from rest_framework.test import APIClient
from .models import Product

class ProductTests(TestCase):
    def setUp(self):
```

```
        self.client = APIClient()

        self.product = Product.objects.create(name='Test
Product', price=10.00, description='Test Description')

    def test_get_products(self):

        url = reverse('product-list-create')

        response = self.client.get(url)

        self.assertEqual(response.status_code,
status.HTTP_200_OK)

        self.assertEqual(len(response.data), 1)
```

7. Documentation: Document your API endpoints using tools provided by DRF, such as the browsable API or third-party documentation generators.

```python
# urls.py

from django.urls import path, include

from rest_framework.documentation import include_docs_urls

urlpatterns = [
```

        path('api/docs/', include_docs_urls(title='API Documentation')),

    # Other API URL patterns
```

By following these steps, you can build a RESTful API with Django and DRF that exposes CRUD operations for managing products. Django's rich ecosystem and DRF's powerful features make it easy to develop APIs that adhere to RESTful principles and provide a seamless experience for clients consuming the API.

Django is a versatile web framework that empowers developers to build web applications and APIs quickly and efficiently. With its built-in features, robust ecosystem, and adherence to best practices, Django is an excellent choice for projects of all sizes and complexities. Whether you're building a simple web application or a complex API-driven system, Django provides the tools and conventions necessary to bring your ideas to life.

## Essential Django Concepts: Models, Views, and URLs

Django, a high-level Python web framework, revolves around three core concepts: models, views, and URLs. Understanding these concepts is essential for building web applications and RESTful APIs with Django. In this guide, we'll delve into each of these concepts, explore
```

their significance, and provide practical examples to illustrate how they work together to create powerful web applications.

1. Models

Models in Django represent the structure of the application's data and are typically defined using Python classes. Django's Object-Relational Mapping (ORM) system abstracts away the complexities of database interactions, allowing developers to interact with the database using high-level Python objects rather than raw SQL queries. Models define the fields and behavior of the application's data, including relationships between different entities.

Example:

```python
# models.py

from django.db import models

class Product(models.Model):
    name = models.CharField(max_length=100)
    price = models.DecimalField(max_digits=10, decimal_places=2)
    description = models.TextField()
```

```
    def __str__(self):
        return self.name
```

In this example, we define a `Product` model with three fields: `name`, `price`, and `description`. Each field is represented by a corresponding Django field type (`CharField`, `DecimalField`, `TextField`). The `__str__` method provides a human-readable representation of the model instance, which is useful for debugging and displaying objects in the Django admin interface.

2. Views

Views in Django encapsulate the logic for processing HTTP requests and generating HTTP responses. Views receive incoming requests from clients, perform any necessary processing (such as querying the database or invoking business logic), and return an HTTP response, typically in the form of HTML content or serialized data (e.g., JSON or XML). Views can be implemented as functions or classes, depending on the complexity of the logic involved.

Example:

```python
# views.py

from django.shortcuts import render
from django.http import JsonResponse
from .models import Product

def product_list(request):
    products = Product.objects.all()
    data = [{'name': product.name, 'price': product.price} for product in products]
    return JsonResponse(data, safe=False)
```

In this example, we define a `product_list` view function that queries all products from the database using the `Product.objects.all()` method. We then serialize the product data into a JSON response using a list comprehension and return it using Django's `JsonResponse` class.

3. URLs

URLs in Django map incoming HTTP requests to corresponding views within the application. Django's URL routing system allows developers to define URL patterns that match specific patterns or patterns with dynamic segments (e.g., `<int:pk>` for a numeric identifier). URL patterns are defined using regular expressions or simple string patterns and are typically organized in a centralized URL configuration file.

Example:

```python
# urls.py

from django.urls import path
from . import views

urlpatterns = [
    path('products/', views.product_list, name='product-list'),
]
```

In this example, we define a URL pattern that maps requests to the `/products/` endpoint to the `product_list` view function. The `name` parameter provides a unique identifier for the URL pattern, which can be referenced in other parts of the Django application, such as templates or view functions.

Putting It All Together

Now that we've covered the essential Django concepts of models, views, and URLs, let's see how they work together to build a simple web application:

1. Define Models: Define one or more Django models to represent the application's data structure, including fields and relationships.

2. Implement Views: Implement view functions or classes to process incoming HTTP requests, perform any necessary data processing, and generate HTTP responses.

3. Configure URLs: Define URL patterns in a centralized URL configuration file (`urls.py`) to map incoming requests to corresponding views.

Example:

```python
# models.py

from django.db import models

class Product(models.Model):
    name = models.CharField(max_length=100)
    price = models.DecimalField(max_digits=10, decimal_places=2)
```

```python
    description = models.TextField()

    def __str__(self):
        return self.name
```

```python
# views.py

from django.shortcuts import render
from django.http import JsonResponse
from .models import Product

def product_list(request):
    products = Product.objects.all()
    data = [{'name': product.name, 'price': product.price} for product in products]
    return JsonResponse(data, safe=False)
```

```python
# urls.py

from django.urls import path
from . import views

urlpatterns = [
    path('products/', views.product_list, name='product-list'),
]
```

```

In this example, we define a `Product` model representing a product in an e-commerce application. We then implement a `product_list` view function that queries all products from the database and returns a JSON response containing the product data. Finally, we define a URL pattern that maps requests to the `/products/` endpoint to the `product_list` view function.

By following these steps and leveraging Django's models, views, and URLs, developers can build robust and scalable web applications and APIs with ease. Django's pragmatic approach to web development and its rich ecosystem of libraries and tools make it an ideal choice for projects of all sizes and complexities. Whether you're building a simple blog or a complex e-commerce platform, Django provides the tools and conventions necessary to bring your ideas to life.

### Setting Up Your Django Development Environment: Let's Get Coding!

Setting up a Django development environment is the first step towards building web applications and RESTful APIs with Django. A well-configured development environment ensures a smooth and efficient development process, allowing developers to focus on writing code
```

and building features. In this guide, we'll walk through the steps to set up your Django development environment, covering everything from installing Django and setting up a virtual environment to configuring your project structure and running your first Django server.

1. Install Python

Django is a Python web framework, so the first step is to ensure you have Python installed on your system. You can download and install Python from the official Python website (https://www.python.org/). Make sure to install a version of Python that is supported by Django (typically Python 3.6 or higher).

2. Set Up a Virtual Environment

A virtual environment is a self-contained directory that contains a Python installation for a particular version of Python, as well as a separate set of installed packages. Using virtual environments is recommended to avoid conflicts between different projects and to maintain project dependencies. You can create a virtual environment using the following commands:

```bash
# Install virtualenv if you haven't already
pip install virtualenv
```

```
# Create a new virtual environment
virtualenv myenv

# Activate the virtual environment
# On Windows
myenv\Scripts\activate
# On macOS/Linux
source myenv/bin/activate
```

3. Install Django

Once you've activated your virtual environment, you can install Django using pip, Python's package manager.

```bash
pip install django
```

This will install the latest version of Django. If you want to install a specific version, you can specify it like this:

```bash
pip install django==3.2.4
```

4. Create a Django Project

Now that Django is installed, you can create a new Django project using the `django-admin` command-line utility.

```bash
django-admin startproject myproject
```

This will create a new directory called `myproject` containing the initial project structure for your Django project.

5. Create a Django App

In Django, applications are modular components that encapsulate specific functionality. You can create a new Django app within your project using the `manage.py` utility.

```bash
cd myproject
python manage.py startapp myapp
```

This will create a new directory called `myapp` containing the files and folders for your Django app.

6. Define Models

Models in Django represent the structure of the application's data. You can define models in the `models.py` file within your app directory.

```python
# myapp/models.py

from django.db import models

class Product(models.Model):
    name = models.CharField(max_length=100)
    price = models.DecimalField(max_digits=10, decimal_places=2)
    description = models.TextField()

    def __str__(self):
        return self.name
```

7. Configure Settings

Django's settings file (`settings.py`) contains configuration settings for your project, such as database settings, installed apps, and middleware.

```python
```

```
# myproject/settings.py

INSTALLED_APPS = [
    'django.contrib.admin',
    'django.contrib.auth',
    'django.contrib.contenttypes',
    'django.contrib.sessions',
    'django.contrib.messages',
    'django.contrib.staticfiles',
    'myapp',
]
# Database settings (modify as needed)
DATABASES = {
    'default': {
        'ENGINE': 'django.db.backends.sqlite3',
        'NAME': BASE_DIR / 'db.sqlite3',
    }
}
```

8. Migrate Database

After defining your models, you need to create database tables based on those models using Django's migration system.

```bash
python manage.py makemigrations
python manage.py migrate
```

```

## 9. Create Superuser (Optional)

If you plan to use Django's admin interface, you can create a superuser account to access the admin dashboard.

```bash
python manage.py createsuperuser
```

10. Define Views and URLs

Views in Django handle HTTP requests and generate HTTP responses. URLs map incoming requests to views. You can define views and URLs in the `views.py` and `urls.py` files within your app directory.

```python
# myapp/views.py

from django.shortcuts import render
from django.http import JsonResponse
from .models import Product

def product_list(request):
    products = Product.objects.all()

```
    data = [{'name': product.name, 'price': product.price}
for product in products]
    return JsonResponse(data, safe=False)
```

```python
# myapp/urls.py

from django.urls import path
from . import views

urlpatterns = [
    path('products/', views.product_list, name='product-list'),
]
```

11. Run Django Server

Finally, you can run the Django development server to test your application locally.

```bash
python manage.py runserver
```

This will start the development server, and you can access your Django application by navigating to `http://127.0.0.1:8000/` in your web browser.

Setting up a Django development environment is the first step towards building web applications and RESTful APIs with Django. By following the steps outlined in this guide, you can create a clean and organized development environment and start building your Django projects with confidence. With Django's powerful features and ecosystem, you'll be able to build robust and scalable web applications in no time.

Chapter 3

Demystifying REST: Core Principles for Building Powerful APIs

Understanding RESTful Architecture: Resources, Representations, and Methods

REST (Representational State Transfer) is an architectural style for designing networked applications. RESTful APIs, which adhere to the principles of REST, are commonly used to build web services that allow clients to interact with server resources. In this guide, we'll delve into the key concepts of RESTful architecture, including resources, representations, and methods, and explore how to implement them in Django for building RESTful APIs.

1. Resources

In RESTful architecture, a resource is an abstraction of a piece of data or functionality on the server. Resources are identified by unique URIs (Uniform Resource Identifiers) and can represent entities such as users, products, or documents. Each resource may have multiple representations, such as JSON, XML, or HTML, depending on the client's preferences.

Example:

```python
# urls.py

from django.urls import path
from . import views

urlpatterns = [
    path('products/', views.ProductList.as_view(), name='product-list'),
    path('products/<int:pk>/', views.ProductDetail.as_view(), name='product-detail'),
]
```

In this example, `/products/` and `/products/<int:pk>/` are URIs representing resources in a hypothetical e-commerce application. The `ProductList` and `ProductDetail` views handle requests related to these resources.

2. Representations

A representation is the data associated with a resource at a particular point in time. Representations can take various forms, such as JSON, XML, HTML, or binary data. Clients interact with resources by sending and receiving representations of those resources over the network. RESTful APIs typically support multiple representations to accommodate different client needs and preferences.

Example:

```python
# serializers.py

from rest_framework import serializers
from .models import Product

class ProductSerializer(serializers.ModelSerializer):
    class Meta:
        model = Product
        fields = ['id', 'name', 'price', 'description']
```

In this example, we define a serializer using Django REST Framework to convert `Product` model instances into JSON representations. This serializer allows clients to interact with `Product` resources using JSON data.

3. Methods

HTTP methods, also known as verbs, define the actions that clients can perform on resources. The most commonly used HTTP methods in RESTful APIs are:

- **GET**: Retrieve a representation of the resource.
- **POST**: Create a new resource.
- **PUT**: Update an existing resource.
- **DELETE**: Delete an existing resource.

These methods correspond to CRUD (Create, Read, Update, Delete) operations and are used to manipulate resources in a RESTful manner.

Example:

```python
# views.py

from rest_framework import generics
from .models import Product
from .serializers import ProductSerializer

class ProductList(generics.ListCreateAPIView):
    queryset = Product.objects.all()
    serializer_class = ProductSerializer
```

```
class ProductDetail(generics.RetrieveUpdateDestroyAPIView):
    queryset = Product.objects.all()
    serializer_class = ProductSerializer
```

In this example, we define two views using Django REST Framework's `generics` class-based views: `ProductList` and `ProductDetail`. The `ProductList` view supports GET (list) and POST (create) operations, while the `ProductDetail` view supports GET (retrieve), PUT (update), and DELETE (destroy) operations.

Implementing RESTful APIs with Django

To implement RESTful APIs in Django, you can follow these steps:

1. Define models representing your application's data.

2. Create serializers to convert model instances into representations suitable for clients.

3. Implement views to handle HTTP requests and generate HTTP responses.

4. Define URL patterns to map incoming requests to views.

5. Optionally, implement authentication, permissions, and pagination to secure and optimize your APIs.

Example:

```python
# models.py

from django.db import models

class Product(models.Model):
    name = models.CharField(max_length=100)
    price = models.DecimalField(max_digits=10, decimal_places=2)
    description = models.TextField()

    def __str__(self):
        return self.name
```

```python
# serializers.py

from rest_framework import serializers
from .models import Product
```

```python
class ProductSerializer(serializers.ModelSerializer):
    class Meta:
        model = Product
        fields = ['id', 'name', 'price', 'description']
```

```python
# views.py

from rest_framework import generics
from .models import Product
from .serializers import ProductSerializer

class ProductList(generics.ListCreateAPIView):
    queryset = Product.objects.all()
    serializer_class = ProductSerializer

class ProductDetail(generics.RetrieveUpdateDestroyAPIView):
    queryset = Product.objects.all()
    serializer_class = ProductSerializer
```

```python
# urls.py

from django.urls import path
from . import views
```

```
urlpatterns = [
    path('products/', views.ProductList.as_view(), name='product-list'),
    path('products/<int:pk>/', views.ProductDetail.as_view(), name='product-detail'),
]
```

Understanding the key concepts of RESTful architecture—resources, representations, and methods—is essential for building scalable and maintainable web APIs with Django. By following RESTful principles and leveraging Django and Django REST Framework, you can design APIs that are flexible, efficient, and interoperable with a wide range of clients. Whether you're building a simple CRUD API or a complex web service, RESTful architecture provides a solid foundation for designing robust and scalable systems.

HTTP Methods in RESTful APIs: GET, POST, PUT, DELETE, and Beyond

HTTP methods play a crucial role in RESTful APIs, defining the actions that clients can perform on resources. Each HTTP method corresponds to a specific operation, allowing clients to retrieve, create, update, and delete resources in a standardized and uniform manner. In this guide, we'll explore the most common

HTTP methods used in RESTful APIs—GET, POST, PUT, and DELETE—and delve into how to implement them in Django for building robust and scalable APIs.

1. GET Method

The GET method is used to retrieve a representation of a resource from the server. It is a safe and idempotent operation, meaning that multiple identical requests will produce the same result, and it does not modify the state of the server.

Example:

```python
# views.py

from rest_framework import generics
from .models import Product
from .serializers import ProductSerializer

class ProductList(generics.ListAPIView):
    queryset = Product.objects.all()
    serializer_class = ProductSerializer
```

In this example, we define a `ProductList` view using Django REST Framework's `ListAPIView`, which supports GET requests to retrieve a list of products.

2. POST Method

The POST method is used to create a new resource on the server. It submits data to be processed by the server and typically results in the creation of a new resource, with the server assigning a unique identifier to the resource.

Example:

```python
# views.py

from rest_framework import generics
from .models import Product
from .serializers import ProductSerializer

class ProductCreate(generics.CreateAPIView):
    queryset = Product.objects.all()
    serializer_class = ProductSerializer
```

In this example, we define a `ProductCreate` view using Django REST Framework's `CreateAPIView`, which supports POST requests to create a new product.

3. PUT Method

The PUT method is used to update an existing resource on the server. It replaces the entire representation of the resource with the provided data. If the resource does not exist, the server may create it with the provided data and assign a unique identifier.

Example:

```python
# views.py

from rest_framework import generics
from .models import Product
from .serializers import ProductSerializer

class ProductUpdate(generics.UpdateAPIView):
    queryset = Product.objects.all()
    serializer_class = ProductSerializer
```

In this example, we define a `ProductUpdate` view using Django REST Framework's `UpdateAPIView`, which supports PUT requests to update an existing product.

4. DELETE Method

The DELETE method is used to remove a resource from the server. It requests the server to delete the specified resource, resulting in the removal of the resource from the server's database.

Example:

```python
# views.py

from rest_framework import generics
from .models import Product
from .serializers import ProductSerializer

class ProductDelete(generics.DestroyAPIView):
    queryset = Product.objects.all()
    serializer_class = ProductSerializer
```

In this example, we define a `ProductDelete` view using Django REST Framework's `DestroyAPIView`, which supports DELETE requests to delete an existing product.

Beyond CRUD Operations

While GET, POST, PUT, and DELETE are the standard HTTP methods used for CRUD (Create, Read, Update, Delete) operations in RESTful APIs, there are additional methods that can be used for more specific operations:

- **PATCH**: The PATCH method is used to partially update an existing resource. It sends only the data that needs to be updated, rather than the entire representation of the resource.

- **HEAD**: The HEAD method is similar to the GET method, but it requests only the headers of the response, without the body. It is often used to check if a resource exists or to retrieve metadata about the resource.

- **OPTIONS**: The OPTIONS method is used to retrieve the supported HTTP methods and other options for a resource. It allows clients to discover the capabilities of the server without performing any actual operations.

Example:

```python
```

```
# views.py

from rest_framework import generics
from .models import Product
from .serializers import ProductSerializer

class ProductPartialUpdate(generics.UpdateAPIView):
    queryset = Product.objects.all()
    serializer_class = ProductSerializer
```

In this example, we define a `ProductPartialUpdate` view using Django REST Framework's `UpdateAPIView`, which supports PATCH requests to partially update an existing product.

Implementing HTTP Methods in Django

To implement HTTP methods in Django, you can use Django REST Framework's generic class-based views, which provide pre-defined views for handling CRUD operations. By subclassing these views and specifying the appropriate queryset and serializer, you can easily implement the desired HTTP methods for your resources.

HTTP methods are the foundation of RESTful APIs, providing a standardized and uniform interface for clients to interact with server resources. By understanding the semantics of each HTTP method and how to implement them in Django using Django REST Framework, you can design and build robust and scalable APIs that adhere to RESTful principles. Whether you're building a simple CRUD API or a complex web service, HTTP methods provide the necessary tools for creating efficient and interoperable APIs that meet the needs of your clients.

Designing a Clear and Consistent API Structure

Designing a clear and consistent API structure is essential for building robust and maintainable RESTful APIs. A well-designed API structure not only makes it easier for developers to understand and use the API but also enhances its usability, scalability, and interoperability. In this guide, we'll explore the key principles and best practices for designing a clear and consistent API structure using Django for RESTful API development.

1. Define Resource Endpoints

The first step in designing an API structure is to define the resource endpoints that clients will interact with. Resource endpoints represent the entities or objects exposed by the API and correspond to URIs that clients can use to access or manipulate those resources.

Example:

```python
# urls.py

from django.urls import path
from . import views

urlpatterns = [
    path('products/', views.ProductList.as_view(), name='product-list'),
    path('products/<int:pk>/', views.ProductDetail.as_view(), name='product-detail'),
]
```

In this example, `/products/` and `/products/<int:pk>/` are resource endpoints representing a collection of products and individual product instances, respectively. The `ProductList` and `ProductDetail` views handle requests related to these endpoints.

2. Use Consistent Naming Conventions

Consistent naming conventions help make your API more intuitive and easier to understand. Use descriptive and meaningful names for resources, endpoints, query parameters, and request/response fields. Stick to a consistent naming style (e.g., camelCase, snake_case) throughout your API to avoid confusion.

Example:

```python
# serializers.py

from rest_framework import serializers
from .models import Product

class ProductSerializer(serializers.ModelSerializer):
    class Meta:
        model = Product
        fields = ['id', 'name', 'price', 'description']
```

In this example, we use camelCase naming for the serializer fields to maintain consistency with JavaScript conventions.

3. Use HTTP Methods Appropriately

Choose the appropriate HTTP methods (GET, POST, PUT, DELETE, PATCH, etc.) for each endpoint based on the intended operation. Follow RESTful conventions and semantics when selecting HTTP methods to ensure clarity and consistency in API design.

Example:

```python
# views.py

from rest_framework import generics
from .models import Product
from .serializers import ProductSerializer

class ProductList(generics.ListCreateAPIView):
    queryset = Product.objects.all()
    serializer_class = ProductSerializer

class ProductDetail(generics.RetrieveUpdateDestroyAPIView):
    queryset = Product.objects.all()
    serializer_class = ProductSerializer
```

In this example, we use GET and POST methods for the `ProductList` view to retrieve a list of products and create a new product, respectively. We use GET, PUT, and DELETE methods for the `ProductDetail` view to retrieve, update, and delete an individual product.

4. Versioning

Consider versioning your API to provide backward compatibility and support for future changes. Versioning allows you to introduce breaking changes without affecting existing clients and provides a clear mechanism for clients to specify which version of the API they want to use.

Example:

```python
# urls.py

from django.urls import path
from . import views

urlpatterns = [
    path('v1/products/', views.ProductList.as_view(), name='product-list-v1'),
    path('v1/products/<int:pk>/', views.ProductDetail.as_view(), name='product-detail-v1'),
]
```

```

In this example, we prefix the resource endpoints with `/v1/` to indicate the API version. This allows clients to specify the version they want to use when making requests.

## 5. Error Handling

Implement consistent error handling and response formats to provide clear and informative error messages to clients. Use standard HTTP status codes to indicate the outcome of requests and include additional details, such as error codes and messages, in the response body.

**Example**:

```python
# views.py

from rest_framework import status
from rest_framework.response import Response
from rest_framework.views import APIView

class ProductDetail(APIView):
    def get_object(self, pk):
        try:
            return Product.objects.get(pk=pk)

```
        except Product.DoesNotExist:
            raise Http404

    def get(self, request, pk, format=None):
        product = self.get_object(pk)
        serializer = ProductSerializer(product)
        return Response(serializer.data)

    def delete(self, request, pk, format=None):
        product = self.get_object(pk)
        product.delete()
        return Response(status=status.HTTP_204_NO_CONTENT)

    # Implement update method for PUT request
    # Implement partial_update method for PATCH request
```

In this example, we define error handling for the `ProductDetail` view to handle cases where a product with the specified ID does not exist.

6. Pagination and Filtering

Consider implementing pagination and filtering to improve the performance and usability of your API, especially for resource collections with a large number of items. Allow clients to paginate through the results and filter them based on specified criteria.

Example:

```python
# views.py

from rest_framework import generics
from rest_framework.pagination import PageNumberPagination
from .models import Product
from .serializers import ProductSerializer

class ProductPagination(PageNumberPagination):
    page_size = 10
    page_size_query_param = 'page_size'
    max_page_size = 100

class ProductList(generics.ListAPIView):
    queryset = Product.objects.all()
    serializer_class = ProductSerializer
    pagination_class = ProductPagination

    def get_queryset(self):
        queryset = super().get_queryset()
        # Apply filtering based on query parameters
        name = self.request.query_params.get('name')
```

```
    if name:
        queryset =
queryset.filter(name__icontains=name)
    return queryset
```

In this example, we define pagination and filtering for the `ProductList` view. We use Django REST Framework's `ListAPIView` and `PageNumberPagination` classes to paginate the results and limit the number of items per page. We override the `get_queryset` method to apply filtering based on query parameters, allowing clients to filter products by name.

Designing a clear and consistent API structure is essential for building maintainable and user-friendly RESTful APIs. By following best practices such as defining resource endpoints, using consistent naming conventions, choosing appropriate HTTP methods, versioning the API, implementing error handling, and supporting pagination and filtering, you can create APIs that are easy to understand, use, and maintain. With Django and Django REST Framework, you have powerful tools at your disposal to design and build robust and scalable APIs that meet the needs of your clients and users.

Chapter 4

Designing Robust Data Models for Your API using Django Models

In RESTful API development with Django, designing robust data models is crucial for creating a solid foundation for your API. Django's built-in ORM (Object-Relational Mapping) system allows you to define data models using Python classes, making it easy to work with databases and manipulate data. In this guide, we'll explore best practices for designing data models in Django for RESTful APIs, along with practical examples.

1. Define Your Data Models

The first step in designing data models for your API is to define the entities or objects that your API will manage. These entities represent the core data structures of your application and should accurately reflect the underlying domain model.

Example:

```python
# models.py
```

```python
from django.db import models

class Product(models.Model):
    name = models.CharField(max_length=100)
    price = models.DecimalField(max_digits=10, decimal_places=2)
    description = models.TextField()

    def __str__(self):
        return self.name
```

In this example, we define a `Product` model with three fields: `name`, `price`, and `description`. Each field corresponds to a column in the database table representing the `Product` entity.

2. Use Field Types Appropriately

Django provides a variety of field types to represent different types of data, such as integers, strings, dates, and relationships between models. Choose the appropriate field types for each attribute of your data models to ensure data integrity and consistency.

Example:

```python
```

```
# models.py

from django.db import models

class Order(models.Model):
    order_number = models.CharField(max_length=10, unique=True)
    total_amount = models.DecimalField(max_digits=10, decimal_places=2)
    order_date = models.DateTimeField(auto_now_add=True)
```

In this example, we define an `Order` model with fields representing the order number, total amount, and order date. We use `CharField` for the order number, `DecimalField` for the total amount, and `DateTimeField` for the order date.

3. Establish Relationships Between Models

In many cases, your data models will have relationships with other models. Django provides several types of relationships, such as one-to-one, one-to-many, and many-to-many relationships, to represent these associations.

Example:

```python
# models.py

from django.db import models

class Customer(models.Model):
    name = models.CharField(max_length=100)

class Order(models.Model):
    customer = models.ForeignKey(Customer, on_delete=models.CASCADE)
    total_amount = models.DecimalField(max_digits=10, decimal_places=2)
```

In this example, we define a `Customer` model and an `Order` model. Each order belongs to a single customer, so we establish a one-to-many relationship between the `Order` model and the `Customer` model using a foreign key field.

4. Add Constraints and Validation Rules

To ensure data integrity and consistency, you can add constraints and validation rules to your data models. Django allows you to define constraints such as unique constraints, check constraints, and custom validation logic to enforce business rules and prevent invalid data from being saved to the database.

Example:

```python
# models.py

from django.db import models

class Product(models.Model):
    name = models.CharField(max_length=100, unique=True)
    price = models.DecimalField(max_digits=10, decimal_places=2)
    description = models.TextField()

    def clean(self):
        if self.price < 0:
            raise ValidationError("Price must be non-negative.")
```

In this example, we add a unique constraint to the `name` field of the `Product` model to ensure that each product has a unique name. We also override the `clean` method to implement custom validation logic to ensure that the price of the product is non-negative.

5. Consider Performance and Scalability

When designing data models for your API, consider the performance and scalability implications of your design choices. Use efficient data types and indexing strategies to optimize query performance, and denormalize data where necessary to reduce the number of database queries required to retrieve data.

Example:

```python
# models.py

from django.db import models

class Product(models.Model):
    name = models.CharField(max_length=100)
    price = models.DecimalField(max_digits=10, decimal_places=2)
    description = models.TextField()

class Order(models.Model):
    products = models.ManyToManyField(Product)
    total_amount = models.DecimalField(max_digits=10, decimal_places=2)
```

```
    def calculate_total_amount(self):
        return sum(product.price for product in self.products.all())
```

In this example, we denormalize the data by storing the list of products directly in the `Order` model using a many-to-many relationship. This reduces the need for joins when querying orders and can improve query performance, especially for read-heavy workloads.

Designing robust data models is a critical aspect of building RESTful APIs with Django. By following best practices such as defining clear entities, using appropriate field types, establishing relationships between models, adding constraints and validation rules, and considering performance and scalability implications, you can create data models that form a solid foundation for your API. With Django's powerful ORM system, you have the flexibility and tools necessary to design data models that meet the requirements of your application and provide a reliable and efficient data storage solution.

Defining Relationships Between Models: Building Complex Data Structures

In RESTful API development with Django, defining relationships between models is essential for building complex data structures and representing the associations between different entities in your application. Django provides several types of relationships, such as one-to-one, one-to-many, and many-to-many relationships, to model these associations effectively. In this guide, we'll explore how to define relationships between models in Django, along with practical examples and best practices.

1. One-to-One Relationships

One-to-one relationships represent a relationship where each instance of one model is associated with exactly one instance of another model. In Django, you can define a one-to-one relationship using the `OneToOneField` field type.

Example:

```python
# models.py

from django.db import models

class UserProfile(models.Model):
    user = models.OneToOneField(User, on_delete=models.CASCADE)
    bio = models.TextField()
```

```
    avatar = models.ImageField(upload_to='avatars/')
```

In this example, we define a `UserProfile` model with a one-to-one relationship to the built-in `User` model provided by Django. Each `UserProfile` instance is associated with exactly one `User` instance.

2. One-to-Many Relationships

One-to-many relationships represent a relationship where each instance of one model can be associated with multiple instances of another model. In Django, you can define a one-to-many relationship using the `ForeignKey` field type.

Example:

```python
# models.py

from django.db import models

class Author(models.Model):
    name = models.CharField(max_length=100)

class Book(models.Model):
```

```
    author = models.ForeignKey(Author,
on_delete=models.CASCADE)
    title = models.CharField(max_length=100)
    publication_date = models.DateField()
```

In this example, we define an `Author` model and a `Book` model with a one-to-many relationship between them. Each `Book` instance is associated with exactly one `Author` instance, but each `Author` instance can be associated with multiple `Book` instances.

3. Many-to-Many Relationships

Many-to-many relationships represent a relationship where each instance of one model can be associated with multiple instances of another model, and vice versa. In Django, you can define a many-to-many relationship using the `ManyToManyField` field type.

Example:

```python
# models.py

from django.db import models

class Tag(models.Model):
```

```
    name = models.CharField(max_length=50)

class Article(models.Model):
    title = models.CharField(max_length=100)
    content = models.TextField()
    tags = models.ManyToManyField(Tag)
```

In this example, we define a `Tag` model and an `Article` model with a many-to-many relationship between them. Each `Article` instance can be associated with multiple `Tag` instances, and vice versa.

4. Through Relationships

In some cases, you may need to customize the intermediary table used to represent a many-to-many relationship. Django allows you to define a through relationship to specify the intermediary model explicitly.

Example:

```python
# models.py

from django.db import models

class Author(models.Model):
```

```
    name = models.CharField(max_length=100)

class Book(models.Model):
    title = models.CharField(max_length=100)
    publication_date = models.DateField()
    authors = models.ManyToManyField(Author, through='Authorship')

class Authorship(models.Model):
    author = models.ForeignKey(Author, on_delete=models.CASCADE)
    book = models.ForeignKey(Book, on_delete=models.CASCADE)
    role = models.CharField(max_length=50)
```

In this example, we define a `Book` model and an `Author` model with a many-to-many relationship between them, using an intermediary model called `Authorship` to specify additional information about the relationship, such as the author's role.

5. Reverse Relationships

Django automatically creates reverse relationships for ForeignKey and ManyToManyField fields, allowing you to access related objects in the reverse direction.

Example:

```python
# views.py

from rest_framework import generics
from .models import Author
from .serializers import AuthorSerializer

class AuthorDetail(generics.RetrieveAPIView):
    queryset = Author.objects.all()
    serializer_class = AuthorSerializer
```

```python
# serializers.py

from rest_framework import serializers
from .models import Author, Book

class BookSerializer(serializers.ModelSerializer):
    class Meta:
        model = Book
        fields = ['id', 'title', 'publication_date']

class AuthorSerializer(serializers.ModelSerializer):
    books = BookSerializer(many=True, read_only=True)
```

```
    class Meta:
        model = Author
        fields = ['id', 'name', 'books']
```

In this example, we define a `AuthorDetail` view to retrieve details about an author. We use Django REST Framework's `ModelSerializer` to serialize the `Author` model, including the related `Book` instances associated with the author using the reverse relationship.

Defining relationships between models is a fundamental aspect of building complex data structures in Django for RESTful API development. By understanding the different types of relationships available in Django—such as one-to-one, one-to-many, and many-to-many relationships—and how to define them effectively, you can create APIs that accurately represent the associations between different entities in your application. With Django's powerful ORM system and Django REST Framework's serialization capabilities, you have the tools necessary to build robust and scalable APIs that handle complex data structures with ease.

Serializers: Transforming Data into Consumable API Formats

In RESTful API development with Django, serializers play a crucial role in transforming complex data structures into consumable API formats, such as JSON or XML. Serializers handle the conversion of Django model instances into a format that can be easily rendered into JSON, XML, or other content types, and vice versa. In this guide, we'll explore the concept of serializers in Django, how to define serializers for your models, and best practices for using serializers in RESTful API development.

1. What are Serializers?

Serializers in Django are components responsible for converting complex data types, such as Django model instances or querysets, into primitive data types suitable for transmission over the network, such as JSON or XML. Serializers also handle the reverse process of converting primitive data types back into complex data structures.

2. Defining Serializers

In Django, serializers are typically defined using Django REST Framework, a powerful toolkit for building web APIs. You can define serializers by creating classes that inherit from serializers.ModelSerializer or serializers.Serializer, depending on whether you're serializing Django model instances or other types of data.

Example:

```python
# serializers.py

from rest_framework import serializers
from .models import Product

class ProductSerializer(serializers.ModelSerializer):
    class Meta:
        model = Product
        fields = ['id', 'name', 'price', 'description']
```

In this example, we define a ProductSerializer class that inherits from serializers.ModelSerializer. We specify the Product model as the model to be serialized and specify the fields to include in the serialized representation.

3. Serializing Model Instances

To serialize Django model instances, you can use ModelSerializer, which automatically generates serializers based on the model definition. ModelSerializer simplifies the process of defining serializers for models by automatically creating fields for each model field.

Example:

```python
# views.py

from rest_framework import generics
from .models import Product
from .serializers import ProductSerializer

class ProductList(generics.ListAPIView):
    queryset = Product.objects.all()
    serializer_class = ProductSerializer
```

In this example, we define a ProductList view that retrieves a list of Product instances from the database and serializes them using the ProductSerializer.

4. Serializing Nested Relationships

In many cases, your models will have nested relationships, where one model contains references to other models. Django REST Framework provides support for serializing nested relationships using serializers.ModelSerializer and serializers.PrimaryKeyRelatedField.

Example:

```python
# serializers.py

from rest_framework import serializers
from .models import Author, Book

class BookSerializer(serializers.ModelSerializer):
    class Meta:
        model = Book
        fields = ['id', 'title', 'author']

class AuthorSerializer(serializers.ModelSerializer):
    books = BookSerializer(many=True, read_only=True)

    class Meta:
        model = Author
        fields = ['id', 'name', 'books']
```

In this example, we define a BookSerializer and an AuthorSerializer. The AuthorSerializer includes a nested representation of the related Book instances using the BookSerializer.

5. Customizing Serialization Behavior

You can customize the serialization behavior of serializers by overriding methods such as to_representation() or by defining custom serializer fields. This allows you to control how data is represented in the serialized output.

Example:

```python
# serializers.py

from rest_framework import serializers
from .models import Product

class ProductSerializer(serializers.ModelSerializer):
    formatted_price = serializers.SerializerMethodField()

    class Meta:
        model = Product
        fields = ['id', 'name', 'price', 'description', 'formatted_price']

    def get_formatted_price(self, obj):
        return f"${obj.price:.2f}"
```

In this example, we define a ProductSerializer with a custom SerializerMethodField called formatted_price. We override the get_formatted_price() method to return a formatted price string with two decimal places.

6. Deserializing Data

In addition to serializing data, serializers also handle the deserialization of incoming data, converting primitive data types into complex data structures that can be saved to the database.

Example:

```python
# serializers.py

from rest_framework import serializers
from .models import Product

class ProductSerializer(serializers.ModelSerializer):
    class Meta:
        model = Product
        fields = ['id', 'name', 'price', 'description']

    def create(self, validated_data):
        return Product.objects.create(**validated_data)
```

```

In this example, we override the create() method of the ProductSerializer to handle the deserialization of incoming data and create a new Product instance based on the validated data.

Serializers are essential components in RESTful API development with Django, responsible for transforming complex data structures into consumable API formats. By defining serializers for your models, you can control how data is represented in API responses and handle the deserialization of incoming data. With Django REST Framework's powerful serialization capabilities, you have the tools necessary to build robust and scalable APIs that meet the needs of your application and clients.
```

Chapter 5

Understanding Django's URL Routing System for APIs

In Django, URL routing is a fundamental aspect of building web applications and APIs. URL routing refers to the process of mapping URLs to view functions or class-based views that handle HTTP requests and generate responses. In the context of RESTful API development with Django, URL routing plays a crucial role in defining the endpoints of the API and mapping them to the appropriate views for processing. In this guide, we'll explore how URL routing works in Django for API development, along with practical examples and best practices.

1. Basic URL Configuration

In Django, URL routing is typically configured using the urls.py module within each Django app. The urls.py module contains a list of URL patterns defined using the urlpatterns variable. Each URL pattern consists of a regular expression pattern and a view function or class-based view that handles requests to that URL.

Example:

```python
# urls.py

from django.urls import path
from . import views

urlpatterns = [
    path('api/v1/products/', views.ProductList.as_view(), name='product-list'),
    path('api/v1/products/<int:pk>/', views.ProductDetail.as_view(), name='product-detail'),
]
```

In this example, we define two URL patterns—one for listing products (`/api/v1/products/`) and one for retrieving a single product by its primary key (`/api/v1/products/<int:pk>/`). Each URL pattern is associated with a corresponding view class (ProductList and ProductDetail) that handles requests to that URL.

2. Class-based Views for API Endpoints

In Django, views are responsible for processing HTTP requests and returning HTTP responses. For RESTful APIs, views are often implemented using Django's class-based views, which provide a more structured and reusable approach to defining view logic.

Example:

```python
# views.py

from rest_framework import generics
from .models import Product
from .serializers import ProductSerializer

class ProductList(generics.ListCreateAPIView):
    queryset = Product.objects.all()
    serializer_class = ProductSerializer

class ProductDetail(generics.RetrieveUpdateDestroyAPIView):
    queryset = Product.objects.all()
    serializer_class = ProductSerializer
```

In this example, we define two class-based views—ProductList and ProductDetail—using Django REST Framework's generic views. ProductList handles GET requests to list all products and POST requests to create a new product, while ProductDetail handles GET, PUT,

PATCH, and DELETE requests to retrieve, update, and delete a single product.

3. URL Parameters and Path Converters

Django's URL routing system supports the use of URL parameters and path converters to capture dynamic parts of the URL and pass them as arguments to view functions or class-based views.

Example:

```python
# urls.py

from django.urls import path
from . import views

urlpatterns = [
    path('api/v1/products/<int:pk>/', views.ProductDetail.as_view(), name='product-detail'),
]
```

In this example, `<int:pk>` is a path converter that captures an integer value from the URL and passes it as the `pk` argument to the ProductDetail view. This allows the view to retrieve the product with the specified primary key from the database.

4. Namespace and URL Naming

Django allows you to organize URL patterns into namespaces and provide meaningful names for URLs, making it easier to reference and reverse URLs in templates and view functions.

Example:

```python
# urls.py

from django.urls import path
from . import views

app_name = 'products'

urlpatterns = [
    path('api/v1/products/', views.ProductList.as_view(), name='product-list'),
    path('api/v1/products/<int:pk>/', views.ProductDetail.as_view(), name='product-detail'),
]
```

In this example, we define a namespace for the URL patterns using the app_name variable, and we provide names for each URL pattern using the name argument. This allows us to reference and reverse URLs using the namespace and URL names, such as `products:product-list` and `products:product-detail`.

5. Including URLs from Other Apps

Django's URL routing system allows you to include URLs from other apps into the URL configuration of your project, enabling modular and reusable URL patterns across multiple apps.

Example:

```python
# urls.py (project-level)

from django.urls import path, include

urlpatterns = [
    path('api/v1/', include('products.urls')),
    # Other URL patterns...
]
```

In this example, we include the URL patterns from the products app into the project-level URL configuration using the include() function. This allows us to define API endpoints for products in the products app and include them in the project's API URL structure.

Understanding Django's URL routing system is essential for building RESTful APIs with Django. By defining URL patterns, mapping them to appropriate views, and leveraging features such as path converters, namespaces, and URL naming, you can create a well-structured and maintainable API URL structure. With Django's powerful URL routing capabilities, you have the flexibility to design APIs that meet the requirements of your application and provide a seamless experience for clients interacting with your API endpoints.

Defining Resource Endpoints: Mapping URLs to API Functionality

In RESTful API development with Django, defining resource endpoints is crucial for mapping URLs to specific API functionality and providing access to resources over the web. Resource endpoints represent the entities or objects exposed by the API and define the URLs that clients can use to interact with those resources. In this guide, we'll explore how to define resource endpoints in Django for building RESTful APIs, along with practical examples and best practices.

1. URL Patterns and Endpoints

In Django, URL patterns are defined using the urls.py module within each Django app. URL patterns map URLs to view functions or class-based views that handle HTTP requests and generate responses. Resource endpoints are defined as URL patterns that correspond to specific API functionality for accessing and manipulating resources.

Example:

```python
# urls.py

from django.urls import path
from . import views

urlpatterns = [
    path('api/v1/products/', views.ProductList.as_view(), name='product-list'),
    path('api/v1/products/<int:pk>/', views.ProductDetail.as_view(), name='product-detail'),
]
```

In this example, we define two resource endpoints—one for listing products (`/api/v1/products/`) and one for retrieving a single product by its primary key (`/api/v1/products/<int:pk>/`). Each endpoint is associated with a corresponding view class (ProductList and ProductDetail) that handles requests to that URL.

2. Class-based Views for Endpoint Functionality

In Django, views are responsible for processing HTTP requests and generating HTTP responses. For RESTful APIs, views are often implemented using Django's class-based views, which provide a structured and reusable approach to defining view logic for different endpoints.

Example:

```python
# views.py

from rest_framework import generics
from .models import Product
from .serializers import ProductSerializer

class ProductList(generics.ListCreateAPIView):
    queryset = Product.objects.all()
    serializer_class = ProductSerializer
```

```
class ProductDetail(generics.RetrieveUpdateDestroyAPIView):
    queryset = Product.objects.all()
    serializer_class = ProductSerializer
```

In this example, we define two class-based views—ProductList and ProductDetail—using Django REST Framework's generic views. ProductList handles GET requests to list all products and POST requests to create a new product, while ProductDetail handles GET, PUT, PATCH, and DELETE requests to retrieve, update, and delete a single product.

3. Path Parameters for Dynamic Endpoints

In many cases, resource endpoints may include path parameters that capture dynamic parts of the URL and pass them as arguments to view functions or class-based views. Path parameters are specified using path converters in the URL patterns.

Example:

```python
# urls.py
```

```
from django.urls import path
from . import views

urlpatterns = [
    path('api/v1/products/<int:pk>/',
views.ProductDetail.as_view(), name='product-detail'),
]
```

In this example, `<int:pk>` is a path converter that captures an integer value from the URL and passes it as the `pk` argument to the ProductDetail view. This allows the view to retrieve the product with the specified primary key from the database.

4. Query Parameters for Filtering and Pagination

In addition to path parameters, resource endpoints may also accept query parameters to allow clients to filter, paginate, and customize the results returned by the API. Query parameters are passed as key-value pairs in the URL query string.

Example:

```python
# views.py
```

```
from rest_framework import generics
from .models import Product
from .serializers import ProductSerializer

class ProductList(generics.ListAPIView):
    queryset = Product.objects.all()
    serializer_class = ProductSerializer

    def get_queryset(self):
        queryset = super().get_queryset()
        name = self.request.query_params.get('name')
        if name:
            queryset = queryset.filter(name__icontains=name)
        return queryset
```

In this example, we define a ProductList view that retrieves a list of products from the database and filters the results based on the `name` query parameter. This allows clients to filter products by name when accessing the `/api/v1/products/` endpoint.

5. Namespace and URL Naming

Django allows you to organize URL patterns into namespaces and provide meaningful names for URLs, making it easier to reference and reverse URLs in templates and view functions.

Example:

```python
# urls.py

from django.urls import path

app_name = 'products'

urlpatterns = [
    path('api/v1/products/', views.ProductList.as_view(), name='product-list'),
    path('api/v1/products/<int:pk>/', views.ProductDetail.as_view(), name='product-detail'),
]
```

In this example, we define a namespace for the URL patterns using the app_name variable, and we provide names for each URL pattern using the name argument. This allows us to reference and reverse URLs using the namespace and URL names, such as `products:product-list` and `products:product-detail`.

Defining resource endpoints is a fundamental aspect of building RESTful APIs with Django. By mapping URLs to specific API functionality using URL patterns and associating them with appropriate views or class-based views, you can create a well-structured API that provides access to resources over the web. With Django's powerful URL routing system and Django REST Framework's generic views and serializers, you have the tools necessary to define resource endpoints that meet the requirements of your application and provide a seamless experience for clients interacting with your API.

Building RESTful URLs: Aligning with RESTful Design Principles

In RESTful API development with Django, designing and building RESTful URLs is crucial for creating APIs that adhere to RESTful principles and provide a clear and intuitive interface for clients to interact with. RESTful URLs should be resource-oriented, hierarchical, and self-descriptive, allowing clients to understand the structure and semantics of the API endpoints. In this guide, we'll explore how to build RESTful URLs in Django that align with RESTful design principles, along with practical examples and best practices.

1. Resource-Oriented URLs

In RESTful API design, URLs should be resource-oriented, meaning they should represent the entities or objects exposed by the API. Each URL should correspond to a specific resource or collection of resources, and HTTP methods should be used to perform actions on those resources.

Example:

```python
# urls.py

from django.urls import path
from . import views

urlpatterns = [
    path('api/v1/products/', views.ProductList.as_view(), name='product-list'),
    path('api/v1/products/<int:pk>/', views.ProductDetail.as_view(), name='product-detail'),
]
```

In this example, we define two resource-oriented URLs—one for listing products (`/api/v1/products/`) and one for retrieving a single product by its primary key

(`/api/v1/products/<int:pk>/`). Each URL corresponds to a specific resource (products) and allows clients to perform actions such as listing, retrieving, updating, and deleting products.

2. Hierarchical URLs

RESTful APIs often represent resources in a hierarchical structure, with nested URLs representing relationships between resources. Hierarchical URLs help organize the API endpoints and reflect the relationships between different entities in the system.

Example:

```python
# urls.py

from django.urls import path
from . import views

urlpatterns = [
    path('api/v1/categories/', views.CategoryList.as_view(), name='category-list'),
    path('api/v1/categories/<int:category_pk>/products/', views.ProductListByCategory.as_view(), name='product-list-by-category'),
]
```

```

In this example, we define hierarchical URLs for categories and products. The `/api/v1/categories/` endpoint lists all categories, while the `/api/v1/categories/<int:category_pk>/products/` endpoint lists all products belonging to a specific category. This hierarchical structure reflects the relationship between categories and products in the system.

### 3. Self-Descriptive URLs

RESTful URLs should be self-descriptive, meaning they should convey information about the resource they represent and the actions that can be performed on that resource. Self-descriptive URLs make it easier for clients to understand the purpose and semantics of each endpoint without additional documentation.

**Example**:

```python
# urls.py

from django.urls import path
from . import views
```
```

```
urlpatterns = [
    path('api/v1/products/', views.ProductList.as_view(), name='product-list'),
    path('api/v1/products/<int:pk>/', views.ProductDetail.as_view(), name='product-detail'),
]
```

In this example, the URLs `/api/v1/products/` and `/api/v1/products/<int:pk>/` are self-descriptive. The first URL represents the collection of products, while the second URL represents a single product identified by its primary key. The URLs clearly convey the purpose and semantics of each endpoint.

4. Consistent URL Structure

Consistency in URL structure is essential for building a predictable and easy-to-use API. URLs should follow a consistent naming convention and structure across different endpoints, making it easier for clients to navigate and understand the API.

Example:

```python
# urls.py
```

```
from django.urls import path
from . import views

urlpatterns = [
    path('api/v1/products/', views.ProductList.as_view(), name='product-list'),
    path('api/v1/products/<int:pk>/', views.ProductDetail.as_view(), name='product-detail'),
    path('api/v1/categories/', views.CategoryList.as_view(), name='category-list'),
    path('api/v1/categories/<int:category_pk>/products/', views.ProductListByCategory.as_view(), name='product-list-by-category'),
]
```

In this example, all URLs follow a consistent structure (`/api/v1/resource/`), where `resource` represents the name of the resource (e.g., products, categories). Consistency in URL structure makes it easier for clients to predict and construct URLs for different API endpoints.

5. Versioning URLs

Versioning URLs is important for maintaining backward compatibility and allowing clients to evolve independently of the API server. By versioning URLs, you can introduce breaking changes or new features in future versions of the API without affecting existing clients.

Example:

```python
# urls.py

from django.urls import path
from . import views

urlpatterns = [
    path('api/v1/products/', views.ProductList.as_view(), name='product-list'),
    path('api/v1/products/<int:pk>/', views.ProductDetail.as_view(), name='product-detail'),
]
```

In this example, we use the `v1` prefix in the URLs to indicate the version of the API. If backward-incompatible changes need to be introduced in the future, a new version of the API can be created with a different prefix (e.g., `v2`) while maintaining the existing endpoints for backward compatibility.

Building RESTful URLs in Django involves adhering to RESTful design principles such as resource-oriented design, hierarchical structure, self-descriptive URLs, consistent URL structure, and versioning. By following these principles and best practices, you can create APIs that are intuitive, predictable, and easy to use for clients interacting with your API endpoints. With Django's flexible URL routing system, you have the tools necessary to design and implement RESTful URLs that meet the requirements of your application and provide a seamless experience for API consumers.

Chapter 6

Crafting Views in Django for Handling API Requests

In Django, views are responsible for processing HTTP requests and generating HTTP responses. When building RESTful APIs with Django, crafting views involves defining view functions or class-based views that handle API requests, perform business logic, and return appropriate responses. In this guide, we'll explore how to craft views in Django for handling API requests, including practical examples and best practices.

1. Function-based Views

Function-based views are the simplest way to define views in Django. They are Python functions that accept an HTTP request as input and return an HTTP response. Function-based views are suitable for handling basic API functionality and can be defined using Django's `@api_view` decorator when working with Django REST Framework.

Example:

```python
```

```python
# views.py

from rest_framework.decorators import api_view
from rest_framework.response import Response

@api_view(['GET'])
def product_list(request):
    # Retrieve list of products from the database
    products = Product.objects.all()
    # Serialize products data
    serializer = ProductSerializer(products, many=True)
    # Return serialized data as JSON response
    return Response(serializer.data)
```

In this example, we define a function-based view `product_list` using the `@api_view` decorator. The view retrieves a list of products from the database, serializes the data using a serializer, and returns the serialized data as a JSON response.

2. Class-based Views

Class-based views provide a more structured and reusable approach to defining view logic in Django. They are Python classes that inherit from Django's `View` class or Django REST Framework's generic views. Class-based views are suitable for handling more complex API functionality and allow for better organization and code reuse.

Example:

```python
# views.py

from rest_framework import generics
from .models import Product
from .serializers import ProductSerializer

class ProductList(generics.ListAPIView):
    queryset = Product.objects.all()
    serializer_class = ProductSerializer
```

In this example, we define a class-based view `ProductList` using Django REST Framework's `ListAPIView`. The view retrieves a list of products from the database and serializes the data using a serializer. The functionality for listing products is implemented by the generic view, reducing the amount of boilerplate code needed.

3. Handling HTTP Methods

Views in Django can handle different HTTP methods (GET, POST, PUT, PATCH, DELETE) to perform various actions on resources. Function-based and class-based views can define methods corresponding to each HTTP method to handle requests appropriately.

Example:

```python
# views.py

from rest_framework.decorators import api_view
from rest_framework.response import Response
from rest_framework import status

@api_view(['POST'])
def create_product(request):
    if request.method == 'POST':
        # Deserialize request data
        serializer = ProductSerializer(data=request.data)
        if serializer.is_valid():
            # Save validated data to the database
            serializer.save()
            # Return success response
            return Response(serializer.data, status=status.HTTP_201_CREATED)
        # Return error response if data is invalid
```

```
        return Response(serializer.errors,
status=status.HTTP_400_BAD_REQUEST)
```

In this example, we define a function-based view `create_product` to handle POST requests for creating a new product. The view deserializes the request data using a serializer, validates the data, saves the validated data to the database, and returns an appropriate response based on the result.

4. Authentication and Authorization

Views in Django can enforce authentication and authorization to restrict access to certain API endpoints. Django REST Framework provides built-in authentication and permission classes that can be applied to views to control access to resources.

Example:

```python
# views.py

from rest_framework.permissions import IsAuthenticated
from rest_framework.authentication import TokenAuthentication
```

```python
class ProductList(generics.ListCreateAPIView):
    queryset = Product.objects.all()
    serializer_class = ProductSerializer
    authentication_classes = [TokenAuthentication]
    permission_classes = [IsAuthenticated]
```

In this example, we define a class-based view `ProductList` with authentication and permission classes applied. The view requires clients to authenticate using a token-based authentication scheme and only allows access to authenticated users.

5. Error Handling

Views in Django should handle errors gracefully and return appropriate error responses to clients. Django REST Framework provides built-in exception handling mechanisms that can be customized to handle errors and return informative error messages to clients.

Example:

```python
# views.py

from rest_framework.exceptions import NotFound
```

```
@api_view(['GET'])
def product_detail(request, pk):
    try:
        product = Product.objects.get(pk=pk)
        serializer = ProductSerializer(product)
        return Response(serializer.data)
    except Product.DoesNotExist:
        raise NotFound(detail="Product not found")
```

In this example, we define a function-based view `product_detail` to handle GET requests for retrieving a single product by its primary key. If the product does not exist in the database, a `NotFound` exception is raised, and an appropriate error response is returned to the client.

Crafting views in Django for handling API requests involves defining view functions or class-based views that perform business logic and return appropriate responses to clients. Whether using function-based views or class-based views, it's essential to handle HTTP methods, enforce authentication and authorization, and handle errors gracefully. By following best practices and leveraging Django's powerful features, you can create robust and scalable APIs that meet the requirements of your application and provide a seamless experience for API consumers.

Processing Data and Performing Operations within Views

In RESTful API development with Django, views play a crucial role in processing data and performing various operations on resources. Views are responsible for handling incoming HTTP requests, processing data, interacting with the database, and returning appropriate responses to clients. In this guide, we'll explore how to process data and perform operations within views in Django for building RESTful APIs, including practical examples and best practices.

1. Retrieving Data

Views in Django can retrieve data from the database using Django's ORM (Object-Relational Mapping) system. This involves querying the database to fetch records that match certain criteria and returning the queried data to clients in the form of HTTP responses.

Example:

```python
# views.py
```

```
from rest_framework import generics
from .models import Product
from .serializers import ProductSerializer

class ProductList(generics.ListAPIView):
    queryset = Product.objects.all()
    serializer_class = ProductSerializer
```

In this example, we define a class-based view `ProductList` that retrieves a list of products from the database using Django's ORM. The `queryset` attribute specifies the queryset used to fetch products, and the `serializer_class` attribute specifies the serializer used to serialize the retrieved data before returning it to clients.

2. Filtering Data

Views in Django can filter data retrieved from the database based on certain criteria specified by clients. This involves applying filters to the queryset used to fetch data, narrowing down the results to only include records that meet the specified criteria.

Example:

```python
# views.py
```

```
from rest_framework import generics
from .models import Product
from .serializers import ProductSerializer

class ProductList(generics.ListAPIView):
    serializer_class = ProductSerializer

    def get_queryset(self):
        queryset = Product.objects.all()
        category_id = self.request.query_params.get('category_id')
        if category_id:
            queryset = queryset.filter(category_id=category_id)
        return queryset
```
```

In this example, we modify the `ProductList` view to filter products based on the `category_id` query parameter. The `get_queryset()` method is overridden to apply a filter to the queryset, narrowing down the results to only include products belonging to the specified category.

### 3. Creating Data
```

Views in Django can create new records in the database by saving data submitted by clients via HTTP requests. This involves deserializing request data, validating it, and saving the validated data to the database.

Example:

```python
# views.py

from rest_framework import generics, status
from .models import Product
from .serializers import ProductSerializer
from rest_framework.response import Response

class ProductCreate(generics.CreateAPIView):
    queryset = Product.objects.all()
    serializer_class = ProductSerializer

    def create(self, request, *args, **kwargs):
        serializer = self.get_serializer(data=request.data)
        serializer.is_valid(raise_exception=True)
        self.perform_create(serializer)
        headers = self.get_success_headers(serializer.data)
        return Response(serializer.data, status=status.HTTP_201_CREATED, headers=headers)
```

In this example, we define a class-based view `ProductCreate` that handles POST requests for creating new products. The `create()` method is overridden to deserialize request data, validate it, and save the validated data to the database. If the data is valid, a success response is returned with status code 201 (Created).

4. Updating Data

Views in Django can update existing records in the database by modifying data submitted by clients via HTTP requests. This involves retrieving the record to be updated, deserializing and validating the updated data, and saving the updated data to the database.

Example:

```python
# views.py

from rest_framework import generics, status
from .models import Product
from .serializers import ProductSerializer
from rest_framework.response import Response

class ProductUpdate(generics.UpdateAPIView):
    queryset = Product.objects.all()
```

```
    serializer_class = ProductSerializer

    def update(self, request, *args, **kwargs):
        partial = kwargs.pop('partial', False)
        instance = self.get_object()
        serializer = self.get_serializer(instance,
data=request.data, partial=partial)
        serializer.is_valid(raise_exception=True)
        self.perform_update(serializer)
        return Response(serializer.data)
```
```

In this example, we define a class-based view `ProductUpdate` that handles PUT and PATCH requests for updating existing products. The `update()` method is overridden to retrieve the product to be updated, deserialize and validate the updated data, and save the updated data to the database. If the data is valid, a success response is returned.

### 5. Deleting Data

Views in Django can delete existing records from the database by removing data submitted by clients via HTTP requests. This involves retrieving the record to be deleted and deleting it from the database.

**Example**:
```

```python
# views.py

from rest_framework import generics, status
from .models import Product
from .serializers import ProductSerializer
from rest_framework.response import Response

class ProductDelete(generics.DestroyAPIView):
    queryset = Product.objects.all()
    serializer_class = ProductSerializer

    def delete(self, request, *args, **kwargs):
        instance = self.get_object()
        self.perform_destroy(instance)
        return Response(status=status.HTTP_204_NO_CONTENT)
```

In this example, we define a class-based view `ProductDelete` that handles DELETE requests for deleting existing products. The `delete()` method is overridden to retrieve the product to be deleted and delete it from the database. If the deletion is successful, a success response is returned with status code 204 (No Content).

Crafting views in Django for handling API requests involves processing data and performing various operations on resources, such as retrieving, filtering, creating, updating, and deleting data. Whether using function-based views or class-based views, it's essential to implement logic to handle different HTTP methods, validate data, interact with the database, and return appropriate responses to clients. By following best practices and leveraging Django's powerful features, you can create robust and scalable APIs that meet the requirements of your application and provide a seamless experience for API consumers.

Building RESTful Views: Implementing GET, POST, PUT, and DELETE Methods

In RESTful API development with Django, views play a crucial role in implementing the functionality for handling HTTP methods such as GET, POST, PUT, and DELETE. These methods correspond to different actions on resources, including retrieving, creating, updating, and deleting data. In this guide, we'll explore how to build RESTful views in Django to implement these HTTP methods, including practical examples and best practices.

1. Implementing GET Method

The GET method is used to retrieve data from the server. In the context of a RESTful API, the GET method is typically used to retrieve a list of resources or a single resource identified by its unique identifier.

Example:

```python
# views.py

from rest_framework import generics
from .models import Product
from .serializers import ProductSerializer

class ProductList(generics.ListAPIView):
    queryset = Product.objects.all()
    serializer_class = ProductSerializer

class ProductDetail(generics.RetrieveAPIView):
    queryset = Product.objects.all()
    serializer_class = ProductSerializer
```

In this example, we define two class-based views—`ProductList` and `ProductDetail`—to handle GET requests for listing all products and retrieving a single product, respectively. The `ListAPIView` and `RetrieveAPIView` generic views provided by Django

REST Framework handle the GET method for listing and retrieving resources.

2. Implementing POST Method

The POST method is used to create new resources on the server. In the context of a RESTful API, the POST method is typically used to submit data to the server to create a new resource.

Example:

```python
# views.py

from rest_framework import generics, status
from .models import Product
from .serializers import ProductSerializer
from rest_framework.response import Response

class ProductCreate(generics.CreateAPIView):
    queryset = Product.objects.all()
    serializer_class = ProductSerializer

    def create(self, request, *args, **kwargs):
        serializer = self.get_serializer(data=request.data)
        serializer.is_valid(raise_exception=True)
        self.perform_create(serializer)
```

```
        headers = self.get_success_headers(serializer.data)
        return Response(serializer.data,
status=status.HTTP_201_CREATED, headers=headers)
```

In this example, we define a class-based view `ProductCreate` to handle POST requests for creating new products. The `CreateAPIView` generic view provided by Django REST Framework handles the POST method for creating resources. The `create()` method is overridden to deserialize request data, validate it, save the validated data to the database, and return a success response with status code 201 (Created).

3. Implementing PUT Method

The PUT method is used to update existing resources on the server. In the context of a RESTful API, the PUT method is typically used to submit data to the server to update an existing resource identified by its unique identifier.

Example:

```python
# views.py

from rest_framework import generics, status
```

```
from .models import Product
from .serializers import ProductSerializer
from rest_framework.response import Response

class ProductUpdate(generics.UpdateAPIView):
    queryset = Product.objects.all()
    serializer_class = ProductSerializer

    def update(self, request, *args, **kwargs):
        partial = kwargs.pop('partial', False)
        instance = self.get_object()
        serializer = self.get_serializer(instance, data=request.data, partial=partial)
        serializer.is_valid(raise_exception=True)
        self.perform_update(serializer)
        return Response(serializer.data)
```
```

In this example, we define a class-based view `ProductUpdate` to handle PUT requests for updating existing products. The `UpdateAPIView` generic view provided by Django REST Framework handles the PUT method for updating resources. The `update()` method is overridden to retrieve the product to be updated, deserialize and validate the updated data, save the updated data to the database, and return a success response with the updated data.
```

4. Implementing DELETE Method

The DELETE method is used to delete existing resources on the server. In the context of a RESTful API, the DELETE method is typically used to submit a request to the server to delete a resource identified by its unique identifier.

Example:

```python
# views.py

from rest_framework import generics, status
from .models import Product
from .serializers import ProductSerializer
from rest_framework.response import Response

class ProductDelete(generics.DestroyAPIView):
    queryset = Product.objects.all()
    serializer_class = ProductSerializer

    def delete(self, request, *args, **kwargs):
        instance = self.get_object()
        self.perform_destroy(instance)
        return Response(status=status.HTTP_204_NO_CONTENT)
```

In this example, we define a class-based view `ProductDelete` to handle DELETE requests for deleting existing products. The `DestroyAPIView` generic view provided by Django REST Framework handles the DELETE method for deleting resources. The `delete()` method is overridden to retrieve the product to be deleted and delete it from the database. If the deletion is successful, a success response with status code 204 (No Content) is returned.

Building RESTful views in Django involves implementing functionality to handle HTTP methods such as GET, POST, PUT, and DELETE for retrieving, creating, updating, and deleting resources. Whether using function-based views or class-based views, it's essential to implement logic to handle each HTTP method appropriately, validate data, interact with the database, and return appropriate responses to clients. By following best practices and leveraging Django REST Framework's powerful features, you can create robust and scalable APIs that meet the requirements of your application and provide a seamless experience for API consumers.

Chapter 7

Guarding Your Fortress: Authentication and Authorization in APIs

Implementing User Authentication Mechanisms for Secure Access

User authentication is a crucial aspect of building secure RESTful APIs with Django. Authentication mechanisms ensure that only authorized users can access protected resources and perform actions within the application. In this guide, we'll explore how to implement user authentication mechanisms for secure access in Django-based RESTful APIs, including practical examples and best practices.

1. Token-based Authentication with Django REST Framework

Django REST Framework (DRF) provides built-in support for token-based authentication, which is a common authentication mechanism for RESTful APIs. Token-based authentication involves issuing a unique token to authenticated users, which they include in subsequent requests to access protected resources.

Example:

```python
# settings.py

REST_FRAMEWORK = {
    'DEFAULT_AUTHENTICATION_CLASSES': [
        'rest_framework.authentication.TokenAuthentication',
```

In this example, we configure DRF to use TokenAuthentication as the default authentication class for all API views. With this configuration, clients must include a valid token in the Authorization header of their requests to authenticate and access protected resources.

2. Generating Authentication Tokens

To authenticate users and generate authentication tokens, Django provides a built-in authentication backend called TokenAuthentication. When a user logs in or registers, a unique token is generated for the user and associated with their account.

Example:

```python
# views.py
```

```
from rest_framework.authtoken.models import Token
from rest_framework.response import Response
from rest_framework.views import APIView

class ObtainAuthToken(APIView):
    def post(self, request, *args, **kwargs):
        username = request.data.get('username')
        password = request.data.get('password')
        user = authenticate(username=username, password=password)
        if user:
            token, created = Token.objects.get_or_create(user=user)
            return Response({'token': token.key})
        return Response({'error': 'Invalid credentials'}, status=400)
```
```

In this example, we define an API view `ObtainAuthToken` to handle authentication requests. When a user provides their username and password in a POST request, the view authenticates the user and generates a token if the credentials are valid. The token is then returned to the client for future authentication.

## 3. Protecting Views with Authentication
```

Once token-based authentication is configured, you can protect views and restrict access to authenticated users by using DRF's authentication classes.

Example:

```python
# views.py

from rest_framework.permissions import IsAuthenticated
from rest_framework.authentication import TokenAuthentication

class ProtectedView(APIView):
    authentication_classes = [TokenAuthentication]
    permission_classes = [IsAuthenticated]

    def get(self, request):
        # Only authenticated users can access this view
        return Response({'message': 'You are authenticated!'})
```

In this example, we define a protected API view `ProtectedView` that requires authentication for access. The view specifies TokenAuthentication as the authentication class and IsAuthenticated as the permission class. Only authenticated users with valid tokens can access this view.

4. Customizing Authentication Backend

Django allows you to customize the authentication backend to implement custom authentication logic if needed. You can create a custom authentication backend by subclassing BaseAuthentication and implementing the authenticate method.

Example:

```python
# authentication.py

from rest_framework.authentication import BaseAuthentication
from django.contrib.auth.models import User

class CustomAuthentication(BaseAuthentication):
    def authenticate(self, request):
        # Custom authentication logic
        username = request.headers.get('X-Username')
        password = request.headers.get('X-Password')
        if not username or not password:
            return None
        try:
```

```
        user = User.objects.get(username=username)
        if user.check_password(password):
            return (user, None)
    except User.DoesNotExist:
        pass
    return None
```

In this example, we define a custom authentication backend `CustomAuthentication` that extracts the username and password from request headers and authenticates users based on this information. This allows for flexibility in authentication mechanisms beyond token-based authentication.

5. Using Third-party Authentication Providers

Django also supports integration with third-party authentication providers such as OAuth 2.0 and social authentication providers (e.g., Google, Facebook, Twitter). You can use packages like `django-allauth` or `python-social-auth` to integrate these authentication providers into your Django application.

Example:

```python
# settings.py
```

```
INSTALLED_APPS = [
    ...
    'allauth',
    'allauth.account',
    'allauth.socialaccount',
    'allauth.socialaccount.providers.google',
]

SOCIALACCOUNT_PROVIDERS = {
    'google': {
        'SCOPE': ['profile', 'email'],
        'AUTH_PARAMS': {'access_type': 'online'},
```

In this example, we configure Django to use Google as a social authentication provider using the `django-allauth` package. Users can authenticate with their Google accounts to access protected resources in the Django application.

Implementing user authentication mechanisms is essential for securing RESTful APIs built with Django. Token-based authentication is a common approach for authenticating users in RESTful APIs, and Django REST Framework provides built-in support for token authentication. By configuring authentication classes and protecting views with appropriate permissions, you can restrict access to authenticated users only. Additionally, Django allows for customization of authentication backends and integration with third-party authentication providers, providing flexibility in implementing authentication mechanisms tailored to your application's requirements. With proper authentication in place, you can ensure that your RESTful API is secure and accessible only to authorized users.

Defining User Permissions and Authorization Levels in Django RESTful APIs

User permissions and authorization levels are essential aspects of building secure and role-based RESTful APIs with Django. Permissions control access to resources and define what actions users are allowed to perform within the application. In this guide, we'll explore how to define user permissions and authorization levels in Django-based RESTful APIs, including practical examples and best practices.

1. Built-in Permissions in Django REST Framework

Django REST Framework (DRF) provides a set of built-in permissions classes that can be used to control access to views and resources based on user roles and permissions. These permissions classes can be applied at the view level or the object level to restrict access to specific resources.

Example:

```python
# views.py

from rest_framework.permissions import IsAuthenticated, AllowAny, IsAdminUser
from rest_framework.views import APIView
from rest_framework.response import Response

class PublicView(APIView):
    permission_classes = [AllowAny]

    def get(self, request):
        return Response({'message': 'This is a public view'})

class ProtectedView(APIView):
    permission_classes = [IsAuthenticated]

    def get(self, request):
        return Response({'message': 'This is a protected view for authenticated users'})

class AdminView(APIView):
```

        permission_classes = [IsAdminUser]

    def get(self, request):
        return Response({'message': 'This is an admin view for admin users'})
```

In this example, we define three API views—`PublicView`, `ProtectedView`, and `AdminView`—each with different permission classes. The `PublicView` allows any user to access it (`AllowAny` permission), the `ProtectedView` requires users to be authenticated (`IsAuthenticated` permission), and the `AdminView` requires users to be admin users (`IsAdminUser` permission).

## 2. Custom Permissions in Django REST Framework

You can also define custom permissions in Django REST Framework to implement fine-grained control over access to resources based on specific business logic or requirements. Custom permissions are defined by subclassing the `BasePermission` class and implementing the `has_permission` method.

**Example**:

```python

```
# permissions.py

from rest_framework.permissions import BasePermission

class IsOwnerOrReadOnly(BasePermission):
    def has_permission(self, request, view):
        return request.user and request.user.is_authenticated

    def has_object_permission(self, request, view, obj):
        if request.method in ['GET', 'HEAD', 'OPTIONS']:
            return True
        return obj.owner == request.user
```

In this example, we define a custom permission `IsOwnerOrReadOnly` that allows users to perform read-only actions (GET, HEAD, OPTIONS) on objects, but only allows the owner of the object to perform write actions (POST, PUT, PATCH, DELETE).

3. Applying Permissions to Views

Permissions can be applied to views by setting the `permission_classes` attribute on the view class or function. You can specify one or more permission classes, and access to the view will be granted if any of the specified permission classes allow the request.

Example:

```python
# views.py

from rest_framework.permissions import IsAuthenticatedOrReadOnly
from .permissions import IsOwnerOrReadOnly

class PostDetail(generics.RetrieveUpdateDestroyAPIView):
    queryset = Post.objects.all()
    serializer_class = PostSerializer
    permission_classes = [IsOwnerOrReadOnly]
```

In this example, we define a view `PostDetail` that allows read-only access to the post detail (`IsAuthenticatedOrReadOnly` permission) and allows write access only to the owner of the post (`IsOwnerOrReadOnly` permission).

4. Dynamic Permission Checks

You can also perform dynamic permission checks based on the request or object being accessed by implementing the `has_permission` and `has_object_permission` methods in custom permission classes.

Example:

```python
# permissions.py

from rest_framework.permissions import BasePermission

class CustomPermission(BasePermission):
    def has_permission(self, request, view):
        # Perform dynamic permission checks based on the request
        if request.user and request.user.is_authenticated:
            # Allow access to authenticated users
            return True
        return False

    def has_object_permission(self, request, view, obj):
        # Perform dynamic permission checks based on the object being accessed
        if obj.owner == request.user:
            # Allow access if the user is the owner of the object
            return True
        return False
```

```

In this example, we define a custom permission `CustomPermission` that performs dynamic permission checks based on the request and the object being accessed. Access is granted if the user is authenticated (`has_permission`) or if the user is the owner of the object (`has_object_permission`).

**5. Setting Default Permissions**

You can set default permissions for all views in your Django REST Framework API by configuring the `DEFAULT_PERMISSION_CLASSES` setting in the Django settings file.

**Example**:

```python
# settings.py

REST_FRAMEWORK = {
    'DEFAULT_PERMISSION_CLASSES': [
        'rest_framework.permissions.IsAuthenticated',
```

In this example, we configure Django REST Framework to use `IsAuthenticated` as the default permission class
```

for all views. This means that by default, views will require users to be authenticated to access them.

Defining user permissions and authorization levels is crucial for building secure and role-based RESTful APIs with Django. Django REST Framework provides a set of built-in permission classes and allows for customization to implement custom permissions tailored to specific business requirements. By applying permissions to views and objects, you can control access to resources and define who is authorized to perform specific actions within the application. With proper permission checks in place, you can ensure that your RESTful API is secure and accessible only to authorized users with the appropriate permissions.

Protecting Your API from Unauthorized Access and Vulnerabilities

Securing a RESTful API is crucial to ensure the integrity and confidentiality of data, as well as to prevent unauthorized access and potential vulnerabilities. In this guide, we'll explore various strategies and best practices for protecting your API from unauthorized access and vulnerabilities using Django, including code examples and practical advice.

1. Enforcing HTTPS Encryption

One of the first and most fundamental steps in securing your API is to enforce HTTPS encryption. HTTPS encrypts the communication between the client and the server, preventing eavesdropping and man-in-the-middle attacks.

Example:

```python
# settings.py

# Ensure that Django uses HTTPS by setting the SECURE_SSL_REDIRECT setting
SECURE_SSL_REDIRECT = True
```

In this example, we configure Django to redirect all HTTP requests to HTTPS by setting the `SECURE_SSL_REDIRECT` setting to `True`. Additionally, ensure that your web server (e.g., Nginx, Apache) is properly configured to support HTTPS.

2. Limiting API Access with API Keys

API keys provide a mechanism for controlling access to your API by requiring clients to include a unique key in their requests. This allows you to track and manage access to your API and prevent unauthorized usage.

Example:

```python
# settings.py

# Define a list of allowed API keys
ALLOWED_API_KEYS = ['your_api_key']

# Middleware to check API key in incoming requests
class ApiKeyMiddleware:
    def __init__(self, get_response):
        self.get_response = get_response

    def __call__(self, request):
        api_key = request.headers.get('Api-Key')
        if api_key not in ALLOWED_API_KEYS:
            return HttpResponseForbidden('Unauthorized')
        return self.get_response
```

In this example, we define a custom middleware `ApiKeyMiddleware` to check for the presence of an API key in incoming requests. Requests without a valid API key are rejected with a 403 Forbidden response.

3. Implementing OAuth 2.0 for Authorization

OAuth 2.0 is a widely-used authorization framework that allows third-party applications to access resources on behalf of users. By implementing OAuth 2.0, you can delegate access control and manage authorization tokens securely.

Example:

```python
# settings.py

INSTALLED_APPS = [

    'oauth2_provider',
]

# OAuth 2.0 configuration
OAUTH2_PROVIDER = {
   'SCOPES': {'read': 'Read access', 'write': 'Write access'},
}

# OAuth 2.0 URL patterns
urlpatterns = [
    ...
```

```
    path('oauth2/', include('oauth2_provider.urls',
namespace='oauth2_provider')),
]
```

In this example, we configure Django to use `oauth2_provider` for OAuth 2.0 support. We define scopes for read and write access and include the necessary URL patterns for OAuth 2.0 endpoints.

4. Rate Limiting API Requests

Rate limiting helps prevent abuse of your API by limiting the number of requests that clients can make within a certain time period. This helps protect your API from denial-of-service (DoS) attacks and ensures fair usage.

Example:

```python
# settings.py

# Django Ratelimit configuration
RATELIMIT_ENABLE = True
RATELIMIT_CACHE = 'default'
RATELIMIT_VIEW = 'django_ratelimit.decorators.cache'
```

```
RATELIMIT_KEY = 'ip'
RATELIMIT_RATE = '5/m'
```

In this example, we configure Django Ratelimit to limit API requests to 5 requests per minute per IP address. Requests exceeding this limit will receive a 429 Too Many Requests response.

5. Input Validation and Sanitization

Ensure that input data from clients is properly validated and sanitized to prevent injection attacks, such as SQL injection and cross-site scripting (XSS). Use Django's built-in validation mechanisms and libraries like Django's forms or serializers to sanitize and validate input data.

Example:

```python
# views.py

from rest_framework import serializers

class CreateUserSerializer(serializers.Serializer):
    username = serializers.CharField(max_length=100)
    password = serializers.CharField(max_length=100)
```

```
    def validate_username(self, value):
        # Ensure username is alphanumeric
        if not value.isalnum():
            raise serializers.ValidationError('Username must be alphanumeric')
        return value
```
```

In this example, we define a serializer `CreateUserSerializer` to validate input data for creating a user. We ensure that the username is alphanumeric to prevent injection attacks.

Protecting your API from unauthorized access and vulnerabilities is crucial to ensure the security and integrity of your application and its data. By enforcing HTTPS encryption, limiting API access with API keys, implementing OAuth 2.0 for authorization, rate limiting API requests, and performing input validation and sanitization, you can mitigate common security risks and prevent potential attacks on your API. Additionally, consider keeping your dependencies up to date, regularly auditing your codebase for security vulnerabilities, and monitoring API usage for suspicious activity. With these measures in place, you can build a secure and reliable RESTful API that meets the needs of your users and protects your application from security threats.
```

Chapter 8

Introduction to API Testing: Guaranteeing Functionality and Reliability

API testing is an essential part of the software development lifecycle, ensuring that APIs function as expected, meet requirements, and maintain reliability. In this guide, we'll explore the importance of API testing, various testing strategies, and how to perform API testing in Django-based RESTful APIs, including practical examples and best practices.

1. Importance of API Testing

APIs serve as the backbone of modern software applications, enabling communication and data exchange between different systems and services. As such, it's crucial to ensure that APIs are thoroughly tested to guarantee functionality, reliability, and compatibility. Here are some reasons why API testing is important:

- **Functionality**: API testing verifies that APIs perform the intended functions and return the expected results for various inputs and scenarios.

- **Reliability**: Testing helps identify and fix bugs, errors, and edge cases that could lead to API failures or unexpected behavior.

- **Compatibility**: APIs need to work seamlessly with different clients, platforms, and environments. Testing ensures compatibility across a wide range of scenarios.

- **Security**: Testing helps identify and mitigate security vulnerabilities, such as injection attacks, authentication issues, and data leaks.

- **Performance**: Testing measures API performance metrics, such as response times, throughput, and scalability, to ensure optimal performance under load.

2. Testing Strategies for RESTful APIs

Testing RESTful APIs involves various strategies and techniques to ensure comprehensive coverage and thorough validation of API functionality. Some common testing strategies include:

- **Unit Testing:** Test individual components of the API, such as models, views, serializers, and utility functions, in isolation.

- **Integration Testing:** Test interactions between different components of the API, such as request handling, data processing, and database operations.

- **Functional Testing:** Test API endpoints and functionality from an end-to-end perspective, simulating real-world usage scenarios.

- **Regression Testing:** Test for unintended side effects or regressions introduced by code changes, ensuring that existing functionality remains intact.

- **Security Testing:** Test for security vulnerabilities, such as injection attacks, authentication bypass, and data exposure, to ensure the API's security posture.

3. Performing API Testing in Django

Django provides a robust testing framework that makes it easy to write and execute tests for Django-based applications, including RESTful APIs. Tests can be written using Django's built-in `unittest` module or third-party testing frameworks like `pytest`. Here's how to perform API testing in Django:

Example:

```python
# tests.py

from django.test import TestCase
from rest_framework.test import APIClient

class APITestCase(TestCase):
    def setUp(self):
        self.client = APIClient()

    def test_get_product_list(self):
        response = self.client.get('/api/products/')
        self.assertEqual(response.status_code, 200)

    def test_create_product(self):
        data = {'name': 'Test Product', 'price': 99.99}
        response = self.client.post('/api/products/', data)
        self.assertEqual(response.status_code, 201)
```

In this example, we define a test case `APITestCase` that inherits from Django's `TestCase` class. We set up an instance of the `APIClient` provided by Django REST Framework in the `setUp` method. We then write test methods to verify the functionality of API endpoints, such as retrieving a list of products and creating a new product.

4. Best Practices for API Testing

To ensure effective and comprehensive API testing, consider the following best practices:

- **Test Coverage:** Aim for high test coverage to validate all aspects of API functionality, including edge cases, error handling, and input validation.

- **Test Data:** Use realistic and representative test data to simulate real-world usage scenarios and ensure thorough testing.

- **Automation**: Automate testing processes as much as possible to reduce manual effort, increase efficiency, and facilitate continuous integration and delivery (CI/CD) pipelines.

- **Isolation**: Test APIs in isolation from external dependencies, such as databases, third-party services, and external APIs, using mocks or fixtures to control test environments.

- **Parameterization**: Use parameterized tests to test API endpoints with different input data, HTTP methods, headers, and query parameters, increasing test coverage and versatility.

- **Assertions**: Use descriptive and meaningful assertions to validate API responses, status codes, data structures, and business logic, providing clear feedback in case of failures.

API testing is crucial for ensuring the functionality, reliability, and security of RESTful APIs in Django-based applications. By adopting appropriate testing strategies, leveraging Django's testing framework, and following best practices, you can effectively validate API functionality, identify and fix bugs, and ensure that APIs meet requirements and expectations. Through comprehensive API testing, you can build robust and dependable APIs that provide a seamless experience for users and clients while maintaining high standards of quality and reliability.

Unit Testing, Integration Testing, and End-to-End Testing for APIs

Testing is an integral part of software development, ensuring that applications meet requirements, perform as expected, and remain reliable over time. When it comes to testing APIs, various types of tests are employed to validate different aspects of API functionality and behavior. In this guide, we'll explore unit testing, integration testing, and end-to-end testing for RESTful APIs developed with Django, including code examples and best practices.

1. Unit Testing for APIs

Unit testing involves testing individual components or units of code in isolation to verify that they work as intended. In the context of API development, unit tests focus on testing functions, classes, and methods responsible for handling specific tasks or operations.

Example:

```python
# tests.py

from django.test import TestCase
from rest_framework.test import APIClient
from .models import Product
from .serializers import ProductSerializer

class ProductTestCase(TestCase):
    def setUp(self):
```

```
        self.product = Product.objects.create(name='Test
Product', price=99.99)
        self.client = APIClient()

    def test_product_model(self):
        self.assertEqual(self.product.name, 'Test Product')
        self.assertEqual(self.product.price, 99.99)

    def test_product_serializer(self):
        serializer = ProductSerializer(instance=self.product)
        self.assertEqual(serializer.data['name'], 'Test
Product')
        self.assertEqual(serializer.data['price'], '99.99')
```

In this example, we define unit tests for the `Product` model and `ProductSerializer`. We use Django's `TestCase` class to set up test data and the `APIClient` to simulate HTTP requests. The `test_product_model` method tests the attributes of the `Product` model, while the `test_product_serializer` method tests the serialization of the `Product` instance using the `ProductSerializer`.

2. Integration Testing for APIs

Integration testing involves testing interactions between different components or modules of an application to ensure that they work together correctly. In the context of API development, integration tests focus on testing the integration between API endpoints, data models, serializers, and other components.

Example:

```python
# tests.py

from django.test import TestCase
from rest_framework.test import APIClient
from .models import Product

class ProductIntegrationTestCase(TestCase):
    def setUp(self):
        self.client = APIClient()
        self.product_data = {'name': 'Test Product', 'price': 99.99}

    def test_create_product(self):
        response = self.client.post('/api/products/', self.product_data)
        self.assertEqual(response.status_code, 201)

        product = Product.objects.get(name='Test Product')
        self.assertEqual(product.price, 99.99)
```

In this example, we define an integration test for creating a product via the API. We use the `APIClient` to send a POST request to the `/api/products/` endpoint with test data. After the request is processed, we verify that the product is created in the database with the correct attributes.

3. End-to-End Testing for APIs

End-to-end testing involves testing the entire application from start to finish to ensure that it behaves as expected in a real-world environment. In the context of API development, end-to-end tests focus on testing the entire API workflow, including client-server interactions, request processing, and response handling.

Example:

```python
# tests.py

from django.test import TestCase
from rest_framework.test import APIClient
from .models import Product

class ProductEndToEndTestCase(TestCase):
    def setUp(self):
```

```
        self.client = APIClient()
        self.product_data = {'name': 'Test Product', 'price': 99.99}

    def test_create_and_retrieve_product(self):
        # Create product
        create_response = self.client.post('/api/products/', self.product_data)
        self.assertEqual(create_response.status_code, 201)

        # Retrieve product
        product_id = create_response.data['id']
        retrieve_response = self.client.get(f'/api/products/{product_id}/')
        self.assertEqual(retrieve_response.status_code, 200)

        # Verify product attributes
        self.assertEqual(retrieve_response.data['name'], 'Test Product')
        self.assertEqual(retrieve_response.data['price'], '99.99')
```

In this example, we define an end-to-end test for creating and retrieving a product via the API. We use the `APIClient` to send a POST request to create the product, then send a GET request to retrieve the product by its ID. Finally, we verify that the retrieved product has the correct attributes.

4. Best Practices for API Testing

When performing unit testing, integration testing, and end-to-end testing for APIs, consider the following best practices:

- **Isolation**: Test components in isolation to ensure that tests are independent and do not interfere with each other.

- **Mocking**: Use mocking libraries to simulate external dependencies, such as databases, third-party services, and external APIs, to control test environments and improve test performance.

- **Parameterization**: Use parameterized tests to test different scenarios, inputs, and edge cases, increasing test coverage and versatility.

- **Data Management:** Set up and tear down test data to ensure that tests start with a clean state and do not leave behind artifacts that could affect subsequent tests.

- **Assertions**: Use descriptive and meaningful assertions to validate expected outcomes and behavior, providing clear feedback in case of test failures.

- **Automation**: Automate test execution and integrate tests into continuous integration and delivery (CI/CD) pipelines to ensure that tests are run consistently and frequently.

Unit testing, integration testing, and end-to-end testing are essential for ensuring the functionality, reliability, and performance of RESTful APIs developed with Django. By employing a combination of these testing strategies and following best practices, you can thoroughly validate API functionality, identify and fix bugs, and ensure that APIs meet requirements and expectations. Through comprehensive API testing, you can build robust and dependable APIs that provide a seamless experience for users and clients while maintaining high standards of quality and reliability.

Utilizing Testing Frameworks for Streamlined Testing Processes

Testing is a critical aspect of software development, ensuring that applications meet requirements, perform as expected, and remain reliable over time. Testing frameworks provide developers with tools and utilities to automate testing processes, streamline testing workflows, and maintain code quality. In the context of RESTful API development with Django, testing frameworks play a vital role in validating API functionality, identifying bugs, and ensuring the overall quality of the API. In this guide, we'll explore the utilization of testing frameworks for streamlined testing processes in Django-based RESTful APIs, including code examples and best practices.

1. Introduction to Testing Frameworks

Testing frameworks provide a structured approach to writing, organizing, and executing tests for software applications. They typically offer features such as test case management, assertion libraries, mocking utilities, and test runners. Testing frameworks help developers write tests efficiently, automate test execution, and integrate tests into continuous integration and delivery (CI/CD) pipelines. In the context of Django-based RESTful APIs, testing frameworks simplify the process of writing and executing tests for API endpoints, serializers, views, models, and other components.

2. Django's Testing Framework

Django comes with a built-in testing framework that provides support for writing and executing tests for Django applications, including RESTful APIs. Django's testing framework offers several features and utilities for testing various aspects of Django applications, such as models, views, forms, and templates. Developers can use Django's testing framework to write unit tests, integration tests, and end-to-end tests for Django-based RESTful APIs, ensuring comprehensive test coverage and reliable API behavior.

Example:

```python
# tests.py

from django.test import TestCase
from rest_framework.test import APIClient
from .models import Product

class ProductTestCase(TestCase):
    def setUp(self):
        self.client = APIClient()
        self.product_data = {'name': 'Test Product', 'price': 99.99}

    def test_create_product(self):
```

```
    response = self.client.post('/api/products/',
self.product_data)
    self.assertEqual(response.status_code, 201)

    product = Product.objects.get(name='Test Product')
    self.assertEqual(product.price, 99.99)
```

In this example, we define a unit test case `ProductTestCase` using Django's `TestCase` class. We set up test data and use Django's test client (`APIClient`) to send a POST request to create a product via the API. We then assert that the response status code is `201` (indicating successful creation) and verify that the product is created in the database with the correct attributes.

3. Pytest Framework

Pytest is a popular testing framework for Python that offers a simpler syntax, powerful features, and extensive plugin ecosystem for testing Python applications, including Django-based RESTful APIs. Pytest provides support for writing concise and expressive tests, fixtures, parametrized tests, and powerful assertions. Pytest can be easily integrated with Django's testing framework, allowing developers to leverage the benefits of both frameworks for testing Django applications effectively.

Example:

```python
# test_views.py

import pytest
from rest_framework.test import APIClient
from .models import Product

@pytest.mark.django_db
def test_create_product():
    client = APIClient()
    product_data = {'name': 'Test Product', 'price': 99.99}

    response = client.post('/api/products/', product_data)
    assert response.status_code == 201

    product = Product.objects.get(name='Test Product')
    assert product.price == 99.99
```

In this example, we define a test function `test_create_product` using Pytest's syntax. We use the `pytest.mark.django_db` decorator to ensure that the test runs in a Django database transaction. We then use an `APIClient` to send a POST request to create a product via the API and assert that the response status code is

`201`. Finally, we verify that the product is created in the database with the correct attributes.

4. Best Practices for Testing Frameworks

When utilizing testing frameworks for streamlined testing processes in Django-based RESTful APIs, consider the following best practices:

- **Consistency**: Choose a testing framework that aligns with your team's preferences, expertise, and project requirements, and stick to it consistently across the codebase.

- **Coverage**: Aim for high test coverage to validate all aspects of API functionality, including edge cases, error handling, input validation, and business logic.

- **Isolation**: Test components in isolation from external dependencies, such as databases, third-party services, and external APIs, using mocks or fixtures to control test environments.

- **Automation**: Automate test execution and integrate tests into CI/CD pipelines to ensure that tests are run consistently and frequently, providing rapid feedback on code changes.

- **Readability**: Write clear, descriptive, and maintainable tests with meaningful test names, comments, and assertions to improve code readability and understandability.

- **Refactoring**: Refactor tests regularly to keep them up to date with changes in the codebase, ensuring that tests remain relevant and reliable over time.

Testing frameworks play a crucial role in facilitating streamlined testing processes for Django-based RESTful APIs, enabling developers to write, execute, and manage tests efficiently. By leveraging Django's built-in testing framework, along with popular third-party frameworks like Pytest, developers can ensure comprehensive test coverage, reliable API behavior, and high code quality. Through consistent application of best practices and continuous improvement of testing processes, developers can build robust and dependable RESTful APIs that meet requirements, perform as expected, and maintain reliability over time.

Chapter 9

Understanding the Need for API Versioning

API versioning is a crucial aspect of API design and development, enabling developers to introduce changes, improvements, and new features to APIs without disrupting existing clients or breaking backward compatibility. In this guide, we'll explore the importance of API versioning, common versioning strategies, and how to implement API versioning in Django-based RESTful APIs, including code examples and best practices.

1. Introduction to API Versioning

API versioning is the practice of managing and maintaining different versions of an API to accommodate changes in functionality, behavior, and data structures over time. As APIs evolve and grow, it's essential to introduce changes in a controlled manner while ensuring that existing clients continue to function as expected. API versioning allows developers to introduce breaking changes, add new features, and deprecate old functionality while providing backward compatibility and support for existing clients.

2. Why API Versioning is Necessary

API versioning is necessary for several reasons:

- **Backward Compatibility:** API versioning allows developers to make changes to APIs without breaking existing clients or requiring them to update their code immediately. Backward compatibility ensures that existing clients continue to function as expected even after changes are introduced.

- **Client Needs:** Different clients may have different requirements, dependencies, and constraints. API versioning allows developers to tailor APIs to meet the specific needs of different clients without impacting other clients.

- **Feature Rollout:** API versioning enables developers to introduce new features gradually, allowing clients to adopt them at their own pace. This approach prevents sudden disruptions and allows for smoother transitions.

- **Bug Fixes and Improvements:** API versioning allows developers to address bugs, performance issues, and usability concerns by releasing updates and improvements to APIs without affecting existing clients.

3. Common API Versioning Strategies

There are several common strategies for API versioning:

- **URL Versioning:** In URL versioning, the API version is included as part of the URL path. For example, `/api/v1/products/` and `/api/v2/products/`. This approach provides clear visibility and control over API versions but can result in cluttered URLs.

- **Query Parameter Versioning:** In query parameter versioning, the API version is specified as a query parameter in the URL. For example, `/api/products/?version=1` and `/api/products/?version=2`. This approach keeps the URL clean but may be less intuitive for developers.

- **Header Versioning:** In header versioning, the API version is specified as a header in the HTTP request. For example, `Accept: application/json; version=1` and `Accept: application/json; version=2`. This approach keeps the URL clean and allows for flexible versioning but may require additional configuration on the client side.

- **Media Type Versioning:** In media type versioning, the API version is specified as part of the media type in the `Accept` header. For example, `Accept: application/vnd.company.product.v1+json` and `Accept: application/vnd.company.product.v2+json`. This approach provides clear versioning semantics but can be more complex to implement.

4. Implementing API Versioning in Django

Django provides several approaches for implementing API versioning:

- **URL Versioning:** In Django, URL versioning can be implemented by defining separate URL patterns for each API version in the `urls.py` module. Each URL pattern maps to a corresponding view or viewset for that version of the API.

```python
# urls.py
```

```python
from django.urls import path
from . import views

urlpatterns = [
    path('api/v1/products/', views.ProductListViewV1.as_view(), name='product-list-v1'),
    path('api/v2/products/', views.ProductListViewV2.as_view(), name='product-list-v2'),
]
```

- **Header Versioning:** In Django, header versioning can be implemented by inspecting the value of a custom header in the request and dispatching requests to the appropriate view or viewset based on the specified version.

```python
# views.py

from rest_framework.views import APIView
from rest_framework.response import Response
from rest_framework import status

class ProductListView(APIView):
    def get(self, request):
```

```
    version = request.headers.get('API-Version')
    if version == '1':
        # Return response for version 1
        return Response({'message': 'Version 1'},
status=status.HTTP_200_OK)
    elif version == '2':
        # Return response for version 2
        return Response({'message': 'Version 2'},
status=status.HTTP_200_OK)
    else:
        return Response({'error': 'Unsupported version'},
status=status.HTTP_400_BAD_REQUEST)
```

5. Best Practices for API Versioning

When implementing API versioning, consider the following best practices:

- **Semantic Versioning:** Follow semantic versioning principles to ensure that API version numbers convey meaning and are consistent with the scope of changes introduced.

- **Documentation**: Provide clear and comprehensive documentation for each API version, including information about changes, deprecations, and migration guides for clients.

- **Deprecation Policy:** Establish a deprecation policy for old API versions, including timelines for deprecation and sunset, to give clients sufficient time to migrate to newer versions.

- **Client Communication:** Communicate changes, updates, and deprecations to clients proactively through release notes, announcements, and developer documentation.

- **Testing**: Test each API version thoroughly to ensure that changes are implemented correctly and do not introduce regressions or compatibility issues.

- **Versioning Strategy:** Choose a versioning strategy that aligns with the needs of your API, the preferences of your development team, and the expectations of your clients.

API versioning is essential for managing changes, improvements, and new features in RESTful APIs developed with Django. By implementing API versioning, developers can introduce changes in a controlled manner, maintain backward compatibility, and provide a seamless experience for clients. Whether through URL versioning, header versioning, or other versioning strategies, API versioning allows developers to evolve APIs over time while ensuring reliability, compatibility, and flexibility. Through adherence to best practices and effective communication with clients, developers can successfully manage API versions and foster a healthy ecosystem of API consumers.

Implementing Versioning Strategies to Maintain Compatibility

Versioning strategies are crucial for maintaining compatibility and managing changes in RESTful APIs. By implementing versioning strategies effectively, developers can introduce new features, fix bugs, and deprecate old functionality without disrupting existing clients or breaking backward compatibility. In this guide, we'll explore various versioning strategies and how to implement them in Django-based RESTful APIs, including code examples and best practices.

1. Introduction to Versioning Strategies

Versioning strategies define how API versions are managed, communicated, and implemented. These strategies help developers introduce changes to APIs in a controlled manner while ensuring backward compatibility and minimizing disruptions for existing clients. Common versioning strategies include URL versioning, header versioning, query parameter versioning, and media type versioning.

2. URL Versioning

URL versioning involves including the API version as part of the URL path. This approach provides clear visibility and control over API versions but can result in cluttered URLs. In Django-based RESTful APIs, URL versioning can be implemented by defining separate URL patterns for each API version in the `urls.py` module.

Example:

```python
# urls.py

from django.urls import path
from . import views

urlpatterns = [
    path('api/v1/products/', views.ProductListViewV1.as_view(), name='product-list-v1'),
    path('api/v2/products/', views.ProductListViewV2.as_view(), name='product-list-v2'),
```

]
```

In this example, we define URL patterns for two API versions (`v1` and `v2`) for the products endpoint. Each URL pattern maps to a corresponding view or viewset for that version of the API.

### 3. Header Versioning

Header versioning involves specifying the API version as a header in the HTTP request. This approach keeps the URL clean and allows for flexible versioning but may require additional configuration on the client side. In Django-based RESTful APIs, header versioning can be implemented by inspecting the value of a custom header in the request and dispatching requests to the appropriate view or viewset based on the specified version.

**Example**:

```python
# views.py

from rest_framework.views import APIView
from rest_framework.response import Response
from rest_framework import status
```
```

```
class ProductListView(APIView):
    def get(self, request):
        version = request.headers.get('API-Version')
        if version == '1':
            # Return response for version 1
            return Response({'message': 'Version 1'}, status=status.HTTP_200_OK)
        elif version == '2':
            # Return response for version 2
            return Response({'message': 'Version 2'}, status=status.HTTP_200_OK)
        else:
            return Response({'error': 'Unsupported version'}, status=status.HTTP_400_BAD_REQUEST)
```
```

In this example, we define a view `ProductListView` that inspects the value of a custom header (`API-Version`) in the HTTP request. Based on the specified version, the view returns a response corresponding to the requested API version.

### 4. Query Parameter Versioning

Query parameter versioning involves specifying the API version as a query parameter in the URL. This approach keeps the URL clean and allows for flexible versioning
```

but may be less intuitive for developers. In Django-based RESTful APIs, query parameter versioning can be implemented by extracting the version from the query parameters and dispatching requests to the appropriate view or viewset.

Example:

```python
# views.py

from rest_framework.views import APIView
from rest_framework.response import Response
from rest_framework import status

class ProductListView(APIView):
    def get(self, request):
        version = request.query_params.get('version')
        if version == '1':
            # Return response for version 1
            return Response({'message': 'Version 1'}, status=status.HTTP_200_OK)
        elif version == '2':
            # Return response for version 2
            return Response({'message': 'Version 2'}, status=status.HTTP_200_OK)
        else:
```

```
        return Response({'error': 'Unsupported version'},
status=status.HTTP_400_BAD_REQUEST)
```

In this example, we define a view `ProductListView` that extracts the API version from the query parameters (`version`). Based on the specified version, the view returns a response corresponding to the requested API version.

5. Media Type Versioning

Media type versioning involves specifying the API version as part of the media type in the `Accept` header. This approach provides clear versioning semantics but can be more complex to implement. In Django-based RESTful APIs, media type versioning can be implemented by inspecting the `Accept` header and dispatching requests to the appropriate view or viewset based on the specified version.

Best Practices for Versioning Strategies

When implementing versioning strategies in Django-based RESTful APIs, consider the following best practices:

- **Consistency**: Choose a versioning strategy that aligns with your API design principles, development workflow, and client expectations, and stick to it consistently across the API.

- **Documentation**: Clearly document how versioning works in your API, including the supported versioning strategies, versioning conventions, and guidelines for clients.

- **Deprecation Policy:** Establish a deprecation policy for old API versions, including timelines for deprecation and sunset, to give clients sufficient time to migrate to newer versions.

- **Testing**: Test each API version thoroughly to ensure that changes are implemented correctly and do not introduce regressions or compatibility issues.

- **Client Communication:** Communicate changes, updates, and deprecations to clients proactively through release notes, announcements, and developer documentation.

Versioning strategies are essential for maintaining compatibility and managing changes in Django-based RESTful APIs. Whether through URL versioning, header versioning, query parameter versioning, media type versioning, or other versioning strategies, developers can introduce changes to APIs in a controlled manner while ensuring backward compatibility and minimizing disruptions for existing clients. By implementing versioning strategies effectively and adhering to best practices, developers can build robust and reliable APIs that evolve over time to meet the needs of clients and users. Through clear documentation, proactive communication, and thorough testing, developers can successfully manage API versions and maintain compatibility, fostering a healthy ecosystem of API consumers and ensuring the longevity and sustainability of their APIs.

Handling Versioning Requests and Maintaining API Stability

Versioning requests and maintaining API stability are essential aspects of developing and managing RESTful APIs. By effectively handling versioning requests and ensuring API stability, developers can introduce changes, updates, and improvements to APIs while preserving backward compatibility and providing a consistent experience for clients and users. In this guide, we'll explore how to handle versioning requests and maintain API stability in Django-based RESTful APIs, including code examples and best practices.

1. Introduction to Handling Versioning Requests

Handling versioning requests involves identifying the requested API version, routing requests to the appropriate version of the API, and responding with the corresponding data format and content. Different versioning strategies, such as URL versioning, header versioning, query parameter versioning, and media type versioning, may be used to specify the desired API version in the request. Regardless of the versioning strategy used, it's essential to implement robust handling mechanisms to ensure that requests are processed correctly and responses are provided in accordance with the requested version.

2. URL Versioning

URL versioning involves including the API version as part of the URL path. In Django-based RESTful APIs, URL versioning can be implemented by defining separate URL patterns for each API version in the `urls.py` module and routing requests to the corresponding views or viewsets.

Example:

```python
```

```
# urls.py

from django.urls import path
from . import views

urlpatterns = [
    path('api/v1/products/', 
views.ProductListViewV1.as_view(), name='product-list-v1'),
    path('api/v2/products/', 
views.ProductListViewV2.as_view(), name='product-list-v2'),
]
```

In this example, we define URL patterns for two API versions (`v1` and `v2`) for the products endpoint. Each URL pattern maps to a corresponding view or viewset for that version of the API.

3. Header Versioning

Header versioning involves specifying the API version as a header in the HTTP request. In Django-based RESTful APIs, header versioning can be implemented by inspecting the value of a custom header in the request and routing requests to the appropriate version of the API.

Example:

```python
# views.py

from rest_framework.views import APIView
from rest_framework.response import Response
from rest_framework import status

class ProductListView(APIView):
    def get(self, request):
        version = request.headers.get('API-Version')
        if version == '1':
            # Handle request for version 1
            return Response({'message': 'Version 1'}, status=status.HTTP_200_OK)
        elif version == '2':
            # Handle request for version 2
            return Response({'message': 'Version 2'}, status=status.HTTP_200_OK)
        else:
            return Response({'error': 'Unsupported version'}, status=status.HTTP_400_BAD_REQUEST)
```

In this example, we define a view `ProductListView` that inspects the value of a custom header (`API-

Version`) in the HTTP request. Based on the specified version, the view routes the request to the appropriate version of the API and returns a response with the corresponding data.

4. Query Parameter Versioning

Query parameter versioning involves specifying the API version as a query parameter in the URL. In Django-based RESTful APIs, query parameter versioning can be implemented by extracting the version from the query parameters and routing requests to the appropriate version of the API.

Example:

```python
# views.py

from rest_framework.views import APIView
from rest_framework.response import Response
from rest_framework import status

class ProductListView(APIView):
    def get(self, request):
        version = request.query_params.get('version')
        if version == '1':
            # Handle request for version 1
```

```
        return Response({'message': 'Version 1'},
status=status.HTTP_200_OK)
    elif version == '2':
        # Handle request for version 2
        return Response({'message': 'Version 2'},
status=status.HTTP_200_OK)
    else:
        return Response({'error': 'Unsupported version'},
status=status.HTTP_400_BAD_REQUEST)
```

In this example, we define a view `ProductListView` that extracts the API version from the query parameters (`version`). Based on the specified version, the view routes the request to the appropriate version of the API and returns a response with the corresponding data.

5. Media Type Versioning

Media type versioning involves specifying the API version as part of the media type in the `Accept` header. In Django-based RESTful APIs, media type versioning can be implemented by inspecting the `Accept` header and routing requests to the appropriate version of the API.

Best Practices for Handling Versioning Requests

When handling versioning requests in Django-based RESTful APIs, consider the following best practices:

- **Consistency**: Choose a versioning strategy that aligns with your API design principles, development workflow, and client expectations, and stick to it consistently across the API.

- **Error Handling**: Implement robust error handling mechanisms to handle requests with unsupported or invalid versions gracefully and provide informative error messages to clients.

- **Fallback Mechanism:** Provide a fallback mechanism or default behavior for requests that do not specify a version, ensuring that clients can still interact with the API without specifying a version explicitly.

- **Documentation**: Clearly document how versioning works in your API, including the supported versioning strategies, versioning conventions, and guidelines for clients.

- **Testing**: Test versioning logic thoroughly to ensure that requests are routed correctly, responses are provided in accordance with the requested version, and error conditions are handled appropriately.

- **Version Discovery:** Implement version discovery mechanisms, such as API introspection or documentation endpoints, to help clients discover available API versions and understand how to interact with them effectively.

Handling versioning requests and maintaining API stability are critical aspects of developing and managing RESTful APIs. By implementing robust versioning mechanisms and adhering to best practices, developers can introduce changes, updates, and improvements to APIs while ensuring backward compatibility and providing a consistent experience for clients and users. Through clear documentation, proactive communication, and thorough testing, developers can successfully handle versioning requests and maintain API stability, fostering a healthy ecosystem of API consumers and ensuring the longevity and sustainability of their APIs.

Chapter 10

The Importance of Clear and Concise API Documentation

Clear and concise API documentation is essential for developers, clients, and users to understand how to interact with an API effectively. Well-documented APIs provide valuable information about endpoints, request and response formats, authentication mechanisms, error handling, and usage guidelines, empowering developers to integrate APIs seamlessly into their applications. In this guide, we'll explore the importance of clear and concise API documentation, best practices for documenting RESTful APIs developed with Django, and how to generate and maintain API documentation effectively.

1. Introduction to API Documentation

API documentation serves as a user manual for developers, providing comprehensive guidance on how to use an API to achieve specific tasks or access certain functionalities. Good documentation enables developers to understand the capabilities and constraints of an API, make informed decisions when integrating the API into their applications, and troubleshoot issues effectively. In the context of RESTful APIs developed with Django, documentation plays a crucial role in facilitating API adoption, fostering collaboration between developers, and promoting the reuse of API resources.

2. Importance of Clear and Concise API Documentation

Clear and concise API documentation offers several benefits:

- **Accessibility**: Documentation makes APIs accessible to a wider audience of developers, regardless of their level of expertise or familiarity with the API. Well-documented APIs lower the barrier to entry and encourage adoption by providing clear instructions and examples.

- **Ease of Integration:** Developers can integrate APIs more efficiently and effectively when they have access to clear and concise documentation. Documentation helps developers understand the API's endpoints, parameters, headers, and response formats, reducing the likelihood of integration errors and misunderstandings.

- **Developer Productivity:** Good documentation saves developers time and effort by providing answers to common questions, explaining usage patterns, and offering troubleshooting tips. Well-documented APIs enable developers to work more productively and focus on building innovative applications.

- **Improved Collaboration:** Documentation fosters collaboration between API providers and consumers by providing a common reference point for communication and understanding. Clear documentation facilitates discussions about API usage, requirements, and enhancements, leading to better outcomes for all parties involved.

- **Reduced Support Overhead:** Comprehensive documentation can help reduce the need for extensive support and assistance from API providers. When developers have access to clear documentation, they can find answers to their questions independently, reducing the burden on support teams and improving overall efficiency.

3. Best Practices for API Documentation

When documenting RESTful APIs developed with Django, consider the following best practices:

- **Use Standard Formats:** Follow established documentation standards and formats, such as OpenAPI (formerly known as Swagger) or API Blueprint, to ensure consistency and interoperability. These formats provide structured ways to describe APIs, including endpoints, parameters, responses, and error codes.

- **Provide Detailed Endpoint Descriptions:** Document each API endpoint thoroughly, including its purpose, supported methods, expected parameters, request/response formats, and example usage scenarios. Use clear and concise language to explain how each endpoint works and what clients can expect from it.

- **Include Usage Examples:** Provide usage examples for each endpoint to illustrate how to construct requests and interpret responses effectively. Real-world examples help developers understand how to use the API in practice and can serve as valuable reference points during integration.

- **Document Authentication Mechanisms:** Explain how authentication and authorization work in the API, including supported authentication methods, token formats, and access control policies. Clearly document how clients can obtain and use authentication credentials to access protected resources.

- **Describe Error Handling:** Document common error scenarios, status codes, and error messages returned by the API. Explain the causes of each error, potential resolutions, and recommended error-handling strategies for clients to follow.

- **Include Code Samples:** Provide code samples in popular programming languages (such as Python, JavaScript, and Ruby) to demonstrate how to interact with the API programmatically. Code samples help developers get started quickly and can serve as valuable reference implementations.

- **Update Documentation Regularly:** Keep API documentation up to date with the latest changes, additions, and deprecations in the API. Regularly review and revise documentation to reflect the current state of the API accurately.

4. Generating API Documentation in Django

Django provides several tools and libraries for generating API documentation automatically from Django REST Framework (DRF) serializers, views, and routers. These tools can parse the API schema and generate interactive documentation that developers can explore in their web browsers. Popular tools for generating API documentation in Django include:

- **DRF-Spectacular:** DRF-Spectacular is a Django REST Framework extension that automatically generates OpenAPI schema and Swagger UI documentation for DRF APIs. It integrates seamlessly with DRF serializers, views, and routers, making it easy to generate and maintain API documentation.

- **Django REST Swagger:** Django REST Swagger is another Django REST Framework extension that generates Swagger/OpenAPI documentation for DRF APIs. It provides a simple decorator-based API for annotating views and generating API documentation in real time.

- **Swagger/OpenAPI Generators:** Swagger/OpenAPI generators, such as Swagger Codegen or OpenAPI Generator, can be used to generate client SDKs, server stubs, and documentation from OpenAPI specifications generated by Django API frameworks.

5. Maintaining API Documentation

Maintaining API documentation is an ongoing process that requires regular review, updates, and improvements. As the API evolves, documentation needs to be updated to reflect changes in endpoints, parameters, response formats, and usage guidelines. It's essential to establish a documentation maintenance workflow and involve API developers, product managers, and technical writers in the documentation review process. Regularly solicit feedback from API consumers and address any gaps, inconsistencies, or inaccuracies in the documentation promptly.

Clear and concise API documentation is essential for developers to understand, integrate, and use RESTful APIs effectively. Well-documented APIs reduce integration friction, improve developer productivity, foster collaboration, and enhance the overall developer experience. By following best practices for API documentation, generating documentation automatically with Django tools, and maintaining documentation regularly, developers can create APIs that are easy to adopt, reliable to use, and valuable to the developer community. Effective API documentation is an investment in the success of the API and the satisfaction of its users, contributing to the growth and sustainability of the API ecosystem.

Utilizing Tools and Standards for Effective API Documentation

API documentation plays a vital role in ensuring that developers understand how to interact with an API effectively. To create comprehensive and user-friendly documentation, developers can leverage various tools and adhere to industry standards. In this guide, we'll explore the importance of utilizing tools and standards for effective API documentation in the context of RESTful API development with Django. We'll also provide examples of how to use these tools and standards to generate high-quality documentation.

1. Introduction to Tools and Standards for API Documentation

Tools and standards for API documentation help streamline the documentation process, ensure consistency, and enhance the overall developer experience. By leveraging these tools and adhering to established standards, developers can create documentation that is easy to understand, navigate, and consume. In the context of Django-based RESTful API development, tools such as Swagger/OpenAPI, Postman, and Sphinx, as well as standards like API Blueprint and RAML, are commonly used to generate and maintain API documentation.

2. OpenAPI/Swagger

OpenAPI, formerly known as Swagger, is a widely adopted standard for describing RESTful APIs. OpenAPI provides a structured way to document APIs using JSON or YAML files, which define endpoints, request and response formats, authentication mechanisms, and other important details. Swagger UI is a popular tool that generates interactive API documentation from OpenAPI specifications, allowing developers to explore and interact with the API in their web browsers.

Example:

```yaml
openapi: 3.0.0
info:
  title: My API
  version: 1.0.0
paths:
  /products:
    get:
      summary: Retrieve a list of products
      responses:
        '200':
          description: A list of products
```

```
      content:
        application/json:
          schema:
            type: array
            items:
              $ref: '#/components/schemas/Product'
components:
  schemas:
    Product:
      type: object
      properties:
        id:
          type: integer
          format: int64
        name:
          type: string
```

In this example, we define an OpenAPI specification for a `/products` endpoint that supports a `GET` method to retrieve a list of products. The specification includes information about the response format, including the JSON schema for the `Product` object.

3. Postman

Postman is a popular API development and testing tool that also offers features for generating API documentation. With Postman, developers can create collections of API requests, organize them into folders, and add descriptions, examples, and tests to each request. Postman can then generate documentation from these collections, including details about endpoints, request parameters, headers, and response formats.

Example:

```json
{
  "info": {
    "_postman_id": "b3e6a37f-51c3-484f-9ad8-35f0d6d61ea3",
    "name": "My API",
    "description": "Documentation for my API",
    "schema": "https://schema.getpostman.com/json/collection/v2.1.0/collection.json"
  },
  "item":
    {
      "name": "Products",
      "description": "Retrieve a list of products",
      "request": {
        "method": "GET",
        "header": [],
        "url": {
```

```
        "raw": "{{baseUrl}}/products",
        "host": ["{{baseUrl}}"],
        "path": ["products"]
      },
      "description": "Get a list of products"
}
```

In this example, we define a Postman collection with a single request to retrieve a list of products. The collection includes details about the request method, URL, and description.

4. Sphinx

Sphinx is a documentation generation tool commonly used in the Python community. While Sphinx is not specific to API documentation, it can be extended with plugins like Sphinx-REST-API to generate API documentation from reStructuredText (reST) files. Sphinx-REST-API allows developers to write documentation in a familiar markup language and generate HTML or PDF output with automatic syntax highlighting, cross-references, and table of contents.

Example:

```rest
```

```
.. http:get:: /products

Retrieve a list of products

**Response**

.. sourcecode:: json
   [
      {"id": 1, "name": "Product 1"},
      {"id": 2, "name": "Product 2"}
   ]
```

In this example, we use reST syntax to document a `GET` request to retrieve a list of products. The documentation includes details about the request method, endpoint, and response format.

5. API Blueprint

API Blueprint is a high-level API description language that allows developers to define RESTful APIs using a concise and human-readable syntax. API Blueprint files are written in Markdown and can be parsed by tools like Aglio or Dredd to generate interactive documentation or perform automated testing. API Blueprint focuses on simplicity and readability, making it easy for developers to write and maintain API documentation without a steep learning curve.

Example:

```markdown
My API

Products [/products]

Retrieve a list of products [GET]

+ Response 200 (application/json)

  + Attributes
    - (array[Product]) products

Data Structures

Product

+ id: 1 (number, required)
+ name: Product 1 (string, required)
```

In this example, we use API Blueprint syntax to define a `/products` endpoint with a `GET` method to retrieve a list of products. We also define the `Product` data structure with attributes for `id` and `name`.

Best Practices for Effective API Documentation

When utilizing tools and standards for API documentation in Django-based RESTful API development, consider the following best practices:

- **Choose the Right Tool:** Select a documentation tool that aligns with your requirements, preferences, and development workflow. Consider factors such as ease of use, integration with existing toolchains, and support for collaboration and versioning.

- **Follow Conventions:** Adhere to established conventions and standards for API documentation, such as OpenAPI/Swagger, API Blueprint, or Sphinx-REST-API. Consistency in documentation format and structure helps developers find information quickly and reduces confusion.

- **Provide Contextual Information:** Include contextual information, such as usage examples, code snippets, and explanations, to help developers understand how to use the API effectively in different scenarios. Contextual information enhances the usability and clarity of the documentation.

- **Keep Documentation Updated:** Regularly review and update API documentation to reflect changes, additions, and deprecations in the API. Outdated documentation can lead to confusion and errors for developers, so it's essential to keep documentation synchronized with the current state of the API.

- **Solicit Feedback:** Solicit feedback from API consumers, developers, and stakeholders to identify areas for improvement in the documentation. Actively seek input on usability, clarity, completeness, and accuracy to ensure that the documentation meets the needs of its audience.

Utilizing tools and standards for effective API documentation is essential for creating documentation that is clear, concise, and user-friendly. By leveraging tools like OpenAPI/Swagger, Postman, Sphinx, and API Blueprint, developers can streamline the documentation process and ensure consistency and accuracy in their API documentation. Following best practices for documentation, such as providing contextual information, keeping documentation updated, and soliciting feedback from stakeholders, helps ensure that API documentation meets the needs of developers and promotes the successful adoption of the API. In the context of Django-based RESTful API development, choosing the right documentation tool and adhering to established standards are key steps in creating documentation that facilitates API integration, collaboration, and usability. By investing time and effort in effective API documentation, developers can enhance the developer experience, reduce integration friction, and contribute to the success of their APIs in the developer community.

Enabling Developers to Easily Understand and Utilize Your API

Creating an API that developers can easily understand and utilize is crucial for its adoption and success. In the world of RESTful API development with Django, there are several strategies and best practices that developers can employ to make their APIs more accessible and user-friendly. In this guide, we'll explore these strategies, provide code examples, and discuss how developers can enable other developers to leverage their APIs effectively.

1. Designing Intuitive and Consistent APIs

One of the fundamental principles of creating an API that is easy to understand and utilize is to design it with simplicity and consistency in mind. This means adopting clear naming conventions, organizing endpoints logically, and ensuring consistency in request and response formats across endpoints. Let's consider an example of designing a simple CRUD (Create, Read, Update, Delete) API for managing products:

```python
# urls.py

from django.urls import path
from . import views

urlpatterns = [
    path('api/products/', views.ProductListCreate.as_view(), name='product-list-create'),
    path('api/products/<int:pk>/', views.ProductRetrieveUpdateDestroy.as_view(), name='product-retrieve-update-destroy'),
]
```

In this example, we define two URL patterns for managing products: one for listing and creating products (`ProductListCreate`) and another for retrieving, updating, and deleting individual products (`ProductRetrieveUpdateDestroy`). By following a consistent naming convention and organizing endpoints logically, developers can easily understand the purpose of each endpoint.

2. Providing Clear and Comprehensive Documentation

Comprehensive documentation is essential for helping developers understand how to interact with an API effectively. Documentation should include information about endpoints, request parameters, authentication mechanisms, response formats, error handling, and usage examples. Using tools like Swagger/OpenAPI or Postman can help generate interactive documentation automatically from API specifications.

Example of API documentation using Swagger/OpenAPI:

```yaml
openapi: 3.0.0
info:
  title: Product API
  version: 1.0.0
paths:
  /products:
```

```
    get:
      summary: Retrieve a list of products
      responses:
        '200':
          description: A list of products
          content:
            application/json:
              schema:
                type: array
                items:
                  $ref: '#/components/schemas/Product'
components:
  schemas:
    Product:
      type: object
      properties:
        id:
          type: integer
          format: int64
        name:
          type: string
        price:
          type: number
```

In this example, the OpenAPI specification defines a `/products` endpoint for retrieving a list of products. The specification includes details about the response format and the `Product` schema.

3. Implementing Descriptive Error Messages

Error messages should be descriptive and informative, providing developers with insights into what went wrong and how to resolve the issue. Error responses should include an appropriate HTTP status code, a clear error message, and, if possible, additional information to help developers troubleshoot the problem. Here's an example of how error messages can be implemented in Django:

```python
# views.py

from rest_framework.views import APIView
from rest_framework.response import Response
from rest_framework import status

class ProductRetrieveUpdateDestroy(APIView):
    def get(self, request, pk):
        try:
            product = Product.objects.get(pk=pk)
            serializer = ProductSerializer(product)
            return Response(serializer.data, status=status.HTTP_200_OK)
        except Product.DoesNotExist:
```

```
        return Response({'error': 'Product not found'}, status=status.HTTP_404_NOT_FOUND)
```

In this example, if a requested product does not exist, the API returns a 404 Not Found response with an error message indicating that the product was not found.

4. Offering Code Examples and Tutorials

Providing code examples and tutorials can significantly aid developers in understanding how to use an API effectively. Examples can demonstrate common use cases, illustrate best practices, and serve as a reference for integrating the API into applications. Code snippets can be included in documentation, README files, or dedicated tutorials on how to get started with the API.

Example of code snippet in documentation:

```markdown
Retrieving a Product

To retrieve information about a specific product, make a GET request to the `/products/{id}/` endpoint, where `{id}` is the unique identifier of the product. Here's an example using Python and the `requests` library:
```

```python
import requests

response = requests.get('https://example.com/api/products/1/')
if response.status_code == 200:
    product_data = response.json()
    print(product_data)
else:
    print(f'Error: {response.status_code} - {response.json()["error"]}')
```

In this example, a code snippet demonstrates how to retrieve information about a specific product using Python and the `requests` library.

5. Supporting Multiple Data Formats and Protocols

To cater to different developer preferences and use cases, APIs should support multiple data formats and protocols for communication. Common data formats include JSON and XML, while popular protocols include HTTP and WebSocket. By offering flexibility in data formats and protocols, APIs can accommodate a wider range of developers and applications.

Example of supporting JSON and XML formats in Django REST Framework:

```python
# serializers.py

from rest_framework import serializers
from .models import Product

class ProductSerializer(serializers.ModelSerializer):
    class Meta:
        model = Product
        fields = ['id', 'name', 'price']
```

In this example, the Django REST Framework serializer supports both JSON and XML serialization out of the box, allowing developers to choose the format that best suits their needs.

Enabling developers to easily understand and utilize an API is essential for its adoption and success. By designing intuitive and consistent APIs, providing clear and comprehensive documentation, implementing descriptive error messages, offering code examples and tutorials, and supporting multiple data formats and protocols, developers can create APIs that are accessible, user-friendly, and developer-friendly. In the context of

RESTful API development with Django, these strategies and best practices can help developers build APIs

Chapter 12

Optimizing Performance for Scalability and High Traffic Volumes

To optimize performance for scalability and high traffic volumes in a RESTful API development environment with Django, we need to consider various aspects of the application architecture, database optimization, caching mechanisms, asynchronous processing, and deployment strategies. Let's delve into each aspect with code examples where applicable.

1. Database Optimization:

Efficient database usage is crucial for handling high traffic volumes. Django provides ORM (Object-Relational Mapping) to interact with databases, but improper usage can lead to performance issues.

a. Indexing:

Indexes speed up database queries by allowing the database engine to quickly locate rows in a table.

```python
from django.db import models
```

```python
class Product(models.Model):
    name = models.CharField(max_length=100)
    price = models.DecimalField(max_digits=10, decimal_places=2)

    class Meta:
        indexes = [
            models.Index(fields=['name']),
```

b. Query Optimization:

Optimize database queries by selecting only required fields and avoiding unnecessary operations.

```python
# Example of selecting specific fields
products = Product.objects.values('name', 'price').all()
```

2. Caching Mechanisms:

Caching frequently accessed data can significantly reduce database load and improve response times.

a. Using Django's Cache Framework:

Django provides a built-in cache framework that supports various caching backends such as Memcached and Redis.

```python
from django.core.cache import cache

# Caching a queryset
products = cache.get('products')
if not products:
    products = Product.objects.all()
    cache.set('products', products, timeout=3600)
```

3. Asynchronous Processing:

Handling long-running or CPU-intensive tasks asynchronously can improve API responsiveness.

a. Using Celery for Asynchronous Tasks:

Celery is a popular asynchronous task queue that integrates well with Django.

```python
from celery import shared_task

@shared_task
```

```
def send_email_task(email, message):
    # Code to send email
    pass

# Invoking the task
send_email_task.delay('example@example.com', 'Hello!')
```

4. Load Balancing:

Distribute incoming requests across multiple server instances to distribute load evenly.

a. Using Nginx for Load Balancing:

Nginx can act as a reverse proxy and distribute requests to multiple Django application servers.

```nginx
upstream django {
    server unix:///path/to/socket.sock;
    server unix:///path/to/another/socket.sock;
}
server {

    location / {
        proxy_pass http://django;
```

}
```

## 5. Horizontal Scaling:

Scaling horizontally involves adding more servers to handle increased traffic.

### a. Deploying Multiple Django Instances:

Deploying multiple instances of the Django application behind a load balancer allows for handling higher traffic volumes.

```bash
# Example deployment using Docker
docker-compose up --scale web=3
```

6. Monitoring and Optimization:

Continuous monitoring and optimization are essential for maintaining optimal performance.

a. Monitoring with Prometheus and Grafana:
```

Prometheus and Grafana can be used to monitor application performance metrics and identify bottlenecks.

b. Performance Testing:

Regular performance testing using tools like Apache JMeter or Locust helps simulate high traffic scenarios and identify performance issues early.

7. Optimizing Django Views and Serializers:

Efficiently written views and serializers can have a significant impact on the overall performance of the Django RESTful API.

a. Use Serializer's `fields` and `exclude` attributes:

When defining serializers, only include necessary fields and exclude unnecessary ones to minimize the data transferred over the network.

```python
from rest_framework import serializers

class ProductSerializer(serializers.ModelSerializer):
    class Meta:
        model = Product
```

```
        fields = ['id', 'name', 'price']  # Only include necessary fields
```

b. Implement Pagination:

Paginate large datasets to limit the number of records returned per API request, reducing response times and database load.

```python
from rest_framework.pagination import PageNumberPagination

class CustomPagination(PageNumberPagination):
    page_size = 10  # Number of records per page
    page_size_query_param = 'page_size'
    max_page_size = 100  # Maximum page size

# In views.py
class ProductListView(ListAPIView):
    queryset = Product.objects.all()
    serializer_class = ProductSerializer
    pagination_class = CustomPagination
```

8. Database Sharding and Replication:

For extremely high traffic applications, consider using database sharding and replication techniques to distribute data across multiple database servers.

a. Database Sharding:

Divide the dataset into smaller, more manageable chunks and distribute them across multiple database servers.

```python
# Example of database routing for sharding
class ShardedRouter:
    def db_for_read(self, model, **hints):
        # Logic to determine which database to read from
        pass

    def db_for_write(self, model, **hints):
        # Logic to determine which database to write to
        pass
```

b. Database Replication:

Replicate the database across multiple servers to distribute read-heavy workloads and improve redundancy.

```python
```

```python
# Example of database replication settings in settings.py
DATABASES = {
    'default': {
        'ENGINE': 'django.db.backends.postgresql',
        'NAME': 'mydatabase',
        'USER': 'mydatabaseuser',
        'PASSWORD': 'mypassword',
        'HOST': 'db1.example.com',  # Master database server
        'PORT': '5432',
    },
    'replica': {
        'ENGINE': 'django.db.backends.postgresql',
        'NAME': 'mydatabase',
        'USER': 'mydatabaseuser',
        'PASSWORD': 'mypassword',
        'HOST': 'db2.example.com',  # Replica database server
        'PORT': '5432',
    }
}
```

Optimizing performance for scalability and high traffic volumes in a Django RESTful API involves a combination of database optimization, caching mechanisms, asynchronous processing, load balancing, horizontal scaling, and continuous monitoring and optimization. By following best practices, implementing efficient code, and using appropriate tools and techniques, you can ensure that your Django application can handle increasing traffic volumes while maintaining optimal performance and scalability.

Caching Strategies, Database Optimization, and Efficient Code Practices

To ensure optimal performance in a RESTful API development environment with Django, it's crucial to implement effective caching strategies, optimize database usage, and follow efficient coding practices. Let's explore each aspect in detail, with code examples where applicable.

1. Caching Strategies:

Caching involves storing frequently accessed data in memory to reduce the need for repeated database queries. Django provides built-in support for various caching backends such as Memcached and Redis.

a. Using Django's Cache Framework:

```python
from django.core.cache import cache

# Caching a queryset
products = cache.get('products')
```

```
if not products:
    products = Product.objects.all()
    cache.set('products', products, timeout=3600)  # Cache for 1 hour
```

b. Cache Decorators:

Django provides cache decorators to cache the output of views or functions.

```python
from django.views.decorators.cache import cache_page

@cache_page(60 * 15)  # Cache for 15 minutes
def my_view(request):
    # View logic
```

2. Database Optimization:

Efficient database usage is crucial for improving performance. Optimizing queries and indexing can significantly reduce database load.

a. Query Optimization:

Optimize queries to select only required fields and minimize database hits.

```python
# Example of selecting specific fields
products = Product.objects.values('name', 'price').all()
```

b. Indexing:

Use indexes to speed up database queries.

```python
class Product(models.Model):
    name = models.CharField(max_length=100, db_index=True)
    price = models.DecimalField(max_digits=10, decimal_places=2)
```

3. Efficient Code Practices:

Writing efficient code can have a significant impact on performance. Follow best practices to ensure clean and optimized code.

a. Serializer Optimization:

When defining serializers, include only necessary fields to minimize data transferred over the network.

```python
class ProductSerializer(serializers.ModelSerializer):
    class Meta:
        model = Product
        fields = ['id', 'name', 'price']  # Only include necessary fields
```

b. Use Generator Functions:

Generator functions can be more memory-efficient than returning large lists or iterators.

```python
def generate_numbers():
    for i in range(1000000):
        yield i
```

4. Utilizing Querysets Wisely:

Django Querysets provide a powerful interface for interacting with the database. Optimizing queryset usage can significantly improve performance.

a. Lazy Evaluation:

Querysets are lazily evaluated, meaning database queries are executed only when the data is accessed. Take advantage of this behavior to defer costly operations until necessary.

```python
# Example of lazy evaluation
queryset = Product.objects.filter(category='Electronics')
# Database query is not executed yet

for product in queryset:
    print(product.name)
# Database query is executed here
```

b. Avoid N+1 Query Problem:

Avoid the N+1 query problem by prefetching related data to minimize the number of database queries.

```python
# Example of prefetch_related
products = Product.objects.prefetch_related('category').all()
```

5. Proper Use of Django Signals:

Django signals allow decoupled applications to get notified when certain actions occur elsewhere in the application. While they are powerful, improper usage can lead to performance issues.

a. Limit Signal Usage:

Avoid excessive use of signals, especially for operations that can be performed synchronously.

```python
from django.db.models.signals import post_save
from django.dispatch import receiver

@receiver(post_save, sender=Product)
def update_product_cache(sender, instance, **kwargs):
    # Update cache or perform other operations
```

6. Minimize Database Hits in Views:

Efficiently written views can minimize database hits and improve overall performance.

a. Use `select_related` and `prefetch_related`:

Use `select_related` and `prefetch_related` to fetch related objects in a single query.

```python
# Example using select_related
queryset = Author.objects.select_related('book').all()

# Example using prefetch_related
queryset = Book.objects.prefetch_related('authors').all()
```

b. Limit Query Results:

Limit the number of results returned by queries to reduce database load and improve response times.

```python
# Example of limiting query results
products = Product.objects.all()[:10]  # Get the first 10 products
```

By implementing caching strategies, optimizing database usage, following efficient coding practices, utilizing querysets wisely, and minimizing database hits in views, you can ensure optimal performance for your Django RESTful API development. It's essential to continuously monitor and profile your application to identify areas for improvement and optimize performance further. With a combination of these techniques and best practices, you can build high-performance RESTful APIs capable of handling large traffic volumes efficiently and reliably.

Ensuring Your API Remains Responsive and Efficient

Ensuring your API remains responsive and efficient is crucial for providing a smooth user experience and handling increasing traffic volumes. In a RESTful API development environment with Django, achieving this involves various strategies, including optimizing code, utilizing asynchronous processing, implementing proper error handling, and employing efficient data serialization techniques. Let's explore each aspect in detail, with code examples where applicable.

1. Optimizing Code:

Efficient code ensures that your API responds quickly to incoming requests and utilizes system resources effectively.

a. Avoiding Nested Loops:

Avoid nesting loops whenever possible, as they can lead to performance bottlenecks, especially with large datasets.

```python
# Example of nested loops
for item in queryset:
    for sub_item in item.related_items:
        # Process sub_item
```

b. Using List Comprehensions:

List comprehensions are often more efficient than traditional for-loops for creating lists.

```python
# Example of list comprehension
squared_numbers = [x**2 for x in range(10)]
```

2. Asynchronous Processing:

Using asynchronous processing allows your API to handle concurrent requests efficiently, improving responsiveness.

a. Using Async Views:

Django 3.1 introduced support for asynchronous views using `async` and `await` keywords.

```python
from django.http import JsonResponse

async def my_async_view(request):
    # Async logic
    return JsonResponse({'message': 'Hello, world!'})
```

b. Asynchronous Task Queues:

Utilize asynchronous task queues like Celery for handling long-running or CPU-intensive tasks asynchronously.

```python
from celery import shared_task

@shared_task
def send_email_task(email, message):
    # Code to send email
    pass

# Invoking the task
send_email_task.delay('example@example.com', 'Hello!')
```

3. Proper Error Handling:

Effective error handling ensures that your API remains resilient and provides meaningful responses to clients.

a. Custom Exception Handling:

Implement custom exception handling to handle errors gracefully and provide informative error messages to clients.

```python
from rest_framework.exceptions import APIException

class CustomException(APIException):
    status_code = 400
    default_detail = 'An error occurred.'
```

b. Global Exception Handling:

Use Django middleware to implement global exception handling and centralize error handling logic.

```python
class CustomExceptionHandlerMiddleware:
    def __init__(self, get_response):
        self.get_response = get_response
```

```python
def __call__(self, request):
    try:
        response = self.get_response(request)
    except Exception as e:
        # Handle exception
        response = JsonResponse({'error': str(e)}, status=500)
    return response
```

4. Efficient Data Serialization:

Efficient data serialization minimizes the amount of data transferred over the network, improving API performance.

a. Selective Field Inclusion:

Include only necessary fields in serialization to reduce response size.

```python
class ProductSerializer(serializers.ModelSerializer):
    class Meta:
        model = Product
        fields = ['id', 'name', 'price']
```

b. Pagination:

Implement pagination to limit the number of records returned per request, reducing response size and improving performance.

```python
from rest_framework.pagination import PageNumberPagination

class CustomPagination(PageNumberPagination):
    page_size = 10
    page_size_query_param = 'page_size'
    max_page_size = 100

# In views.py
class ProductListView(ListAPIView):
    queryset = Product.objects.all()
    serializer_class = ProductSerializer
    pagination_class = CustomPagination
```

5. Rate Limiting:

Implementing rate limiting ensures that your API remains responsive by preventing abuse or excessive usage, thus maintaining a fair distribution of resources among users.

a. Using Django Throttle Classes:

Django Rest Framework provides throttle classes to limit the number of requests that can be made to the API within a certain time period.

```python
from rest_framework.throttling import UserRateThrottle

class MyThrottle(UserRateThrottle):
    rate = '10/day'  # Allow 10 requests per day per user

# In views.py
from rest_framework.decorators import throttle_classes

@throttle_classes([MyThrottle])
def my_view(request):
    # View logic
```

6. Horizontal Scaling and Load Balancing:

Scaling horizontally involves adding more server instances to handle increasing traffic volumes. Load balancing distributes incoming requests across multiple server instances to prevent overloading.

a. Deploying Multiple Django Instances:

Deploy multiple instances of your Django application behind a load balancer to distribute incoming traffic.

```bash
# Example deployment using Docker
docker-compose up --scale web=3
```

b. Load Balancing with Nginx:

Configure Nginx as a reverse proxy to distribute requests among multiple Django application servers.

```nginx
upstream django {
    server unix:///path/to/socket.sock;
    server unix:///path/to/another/socket.sock;
}
server {
    ...
    location / {
        proxy_pass http://django;
    }
}
```

```

## 7. Monitoring and Alerting:

Continuous monitoring and alerting help detect performance issues or failures early, allowing for timely intervention and optimization.

### a. Using Monitoring Tools:

Utilize monitoring tools like Prometheus and Grafana to track key performance metrics such as response time, throughput, and error rates.

### b. Implementing Alerts:

Set up alerts to notify you of abnormal behavior or performance degradation, enabling proactive action to address issues.

```yaml
# Example alert rule in Prometheus
groups:
- name: example
  rules:
  - alert: HighResponseTime
    expr: http_request_duration_seconds > 1
    for: 5m
```
```

    labels:
      severity: warning
    annotations:
      summary: "High response time detected"
      description: "The API response time is higher than normal"
```

Ensuring your API remains responsive and efficient in a Django RESTful API development environment requires a combination of optimization techniques, proper error handling, rate limiting, horizontal scaling, load balancing, and proactive monitoring. By implementing these strategies, you can maintain a high level of performance, even under heavy loads, and provide a reliable and seamless user experience for your API consumers. It's essential to continuously monitor your API's performance, identify areas for improvement, and optimize accordingly to meet the evolving demands of your users.

## Choosing the Right Hosting Platform for Your Production API

Choosing the right hosting platform for your production API is a critical decision that can impact its performance, scalability, reliability, and cost-effectiveness. In this guide, we'll explore various hosting options suitable for hosting a RESTful API developed with Django, along
```

with their pros, cons, and code examples where applicable.

1. Self-Hosting:

Self-hosting involves deploying and managing your API on your own servers or infrastructure. This option provides full control over your environment but requires significant expertise in server management and maintenance.

Pros:

- Complete control over server configuration and resources.

- Ability to customize the environment to suit specific requirements.

- Potential cost savings compared to managed hosting solutions.

Cons:

- Requires expertise in server management, including security updates, backups, and scalability.

- Initial setup and ongoing maintenance can be time-consuming.

- May require significant investment in hardware infrastructure.

Code Example:

```bash
# Example of deploying Django API on self-hosted servers
# Assuming you have Django project ready for deployment

# Install required packages
pip install gunicorn

# Start Django application using Gunicorn
gunicorn my_project.wsgi:application
```

2. Cloud Hosting Providers:

Cloud hosting providers offer scalable and managed infrastructure services, making them a popular choice for hosting production APIs. Providers like AWS, Google Cloud Platform (GCP), and Microsoft Azure offer a wide range of services suitable for hosting Django APIs.

Pros:

- Scalable infrastructure that can handle varying traffic loads.

- Managed services such as databases, load balancers, and monitoring.

- Pay-as-you-go pricing model, allowing for cost optimization.

Cons:

- May have a learning curve for beginners unfamiliar with cloud technologies.

- Pricing can vary based on usage, and costs can escalate if not properly optimized.

- Vendor lock-in may be a concern if relying heavily on proprietary services.

Code Example (Deploying Django API on AWS Elastic Beanstalk):

```bash
# Install AWS CLI and Elastic Beanstalk CLI
```

```
pip install awscli awsebcli

# Initialize Elastic Beanstalk application
eb init -p python-3.8 my-django-api

# Create and deploy Django application
eb create my-django-env
```

3. Platform-as-a-Service (PaaS):

PaaS providers offer pre-configured environments for deploying and managing applications without worrying about underlying infrastructure. Heroku is a popular PaaS provider known for its ease of use and simplicity.

Pros:

- Simplified deployment process with minimal configuration required.

- Automatic scaling and load balancing to handle traffic spikes.

- Built-in support for popular programming languages and frameworks.

Cons:

- Limited control over underlying infrastructure compared to self-hosting or cloud hosting.

- Potential vendor lock-in due to reliance on platform-specific services.

- Costs can add up as usage grows, especially for additional add-ons and services.

Code Example (Deploying Django API on Heroku):

```bash
# Install Heroku CLI
brew tap heroku/brew && brew install heroku

# Login to Heroku
heroku login

# Create Heroku application
heroku create my-django-api

# Deploy Django application
git push heroku master
```

4. Containerization and Orchestration:

Containerization platforms like Docker and orchestration tools like Kubernetes provide a way to package and deploy applications consistently across different environments.

Pros:

- Portability and consistency across development, testing, and production environments.

- Scalability and resilience with built-in features like auto-scaling and rolling updates.

- Flexibility to deploy on-premises or in any cloud environment.

Cons:

- Complexity associated with setting up and managing containerized environments.

- Requires additional knowledge of container orchestration and networking concepts.

- Overhead of managing infrastructure resources for containerized deployments.

Code Example (Deploying Django API on Kubernetes):

```bash
# Create Kubernetes deployment manifest
kubectl create deployment my-django-api --image=my-django-api:latest

# Expose deployment as a service
kubectl expose deployment my-django-api --port=8000 --target-port=8000 --type=LoadBalancer
```

5. Serverless Computing:

Serverless computing abstracts away infrastructure management, allowing developers to focus solely on code development. AWS Lambda, Google Cloud Functions, and Azure Functions are popular serverless platforms suitable for hosting RESTful APIs.

Pros:

- No server provisioning or maintenance required, reducing operational overhead.

- Automatic scaling to handle varying workloads without manual intervention.

- Pay-per-execution pricing model, offering cost savings for low to moderate traffic APIs.

Cons:

- Limited execution time and memory constraints imposed by serverless platforms.

- Cold start latency can impact response times for infrequently accessed APIs.

- Integration with external services may require additional configuration and complexity.

Code Example (Deploying Django API on AWS Lambda with Zappa):

```bash
# Install Zappa
pip install zappa

# Initialize Zappa project
zappa init

# Deploy Django application to AWS Lambda
zappa deploy production
```

6. Content Delivery Networks (CDNs):

CDNs cache and distribute content across a network of servers located worldwide, improving the performance and availability of your API by reducing latency for users across different regions.

Pros:

- Faster response times and improved reliability for global users.

- Offloads traffic from origin servers, reducing load and scaling requirements.

- Built-in security features like DDoS protection and web application firewalls.

Cons:

- May introduce additional complexity and configuration overhead.

- Costs can vary based on usage and traffic patterns, potentially leading to unexpected charges.

- Limited control over caching behavior and cache invalidation strategies.

Code Example (Configuring CDN for Django API with AWS CloudFront):

```bash
# Create CloudFront distribution
aws cloudfront create-distribution --origin-domain-name my-django-api.com --default-root-object index.html

# Update DNS records to point to CloudFront distribution
```

7. Hybrid and Multi-Cloud Deployments:

Hybrid and multi-cloud deployments leverage a combination of on-premises infrastructure, public cloud, and private cloud environments to achieve flexibility, scalability, and redundancy.

<u>Pros</u>:

- Redundancy and fault tolerance across multiple geographically distributed data centers.

- Flexibility to choose the best services from different cloud providers based on specific requirements.

- Avoids vendor lock-in by maintaining flexibility to migrate workloads across different environments.

Cons:

- Increased complexity associated with managing multiple environments and integrating disparate services.

- Potential challenges related to data consistency, latency, and network connectivity between different cloud environments.

- Higher operational overhead for monitoring, troubleshooting, and maintaining hybrid deployments.

Code Example (Deploying Django API on Multiple Cloud Providers):

```bash
# Set up Kubernetes cluster on Google Cloud Platform
gcloud container clusters create my-cluster
```

```
# Deploy Django API on Kubernetes cluster
kubectl create deployment my-django-api --image=my-django-api:latest

# Set up load balancer for Kubernetes cluster
kubectl expose deployment my-django-api --port=8000 --target-port=8000 --type=LoadBalancer
```

Choosing the right hosting platform for your production API involves evaluating various factors such as technical requirements, scalability needs, budget constraints, and preferences for control and flexibility. Whether you opt for self-hosting, cloud hosting, serverless computing, CDN, or hybrid/multi-cloud deployments, each option has its own set of trade-offs. Consider your specific use case, future growth plans, and operational capabilities before making a decision. With the right hosting platform in place, you can ensure that your Django RESTful API is deployed efficiently and reliably to meet the needs of your users while maintaining optimal performance and scalability.

Configuring Your Django Application for Deployment

Configuring your Django application for deployment involves several steps to ensure that it runs smoothly and efficiently in a production environment. This includes settings optimization, security considerations, static files handling, database configuration, and more. Let's dive into each aspect with code examples and best practices for deploying a RESTful API developed with Django.

1. Settings Optimization:

Optimizing Django settings for deployment involves configuring parameters such as DEBUG mode, allowed hosts, database settings, and static file handling.

a. Setting DEBUG Mode:

In production, set `DEBUG` to `False` to disable detailed error pages and enable basic error logging.

```python
DEBUG = False
```

b. Configuring Allowed Hosts:

Specify the list of allowed hosts to prevent unauthorized access to your application.

```python
```

```
ALLOWED_HOSTS = ['yourdomain.com',
'www.yourdomain.com']
```

c. Securing Secret Key:

Store your Django secret key in a secure location, such as an environment variable.

```python
SECRET_KEY = os.environ.get('DJANGO_SECRET_KEY')
```

2. Security Considerations:

Implement security measures to protect your Django application from common vulnerabilities.

a. Using HTTPS:

Always use HTTPS to encrypt data transmitted between clients and your server.

```python
# In settings.py
SECURE_SSL_REDIRECT = True
```

b. Securing Database Credentials:

Avoid hardcoding database credentials in settings.py. Use environment variables or a secure secrets management service.

c. Implementing CSRF Protection:

Enable Cross-Site Request Forgery (CSRF) protection to prevent CSRF attacks.

```python
# In settings.py
CSRF_COOKIE_SECURE = True
```

3. Static Files Handling:

Configure Django to serve static files efficiently in a production environment.

a. Collecting Static Files:

Collect static files into a single directory for serving by a web server.

```bash
```

```
python manage.py collectstatic
```

b. Serving Static Files:

Configure your web server (e.g., Nginx) to serve static files directly, rather than through Django.

4. Database Configuration:

Optimize database settings for production use, including connection pooling, database engine, and caching.

a. Connection Pooling:

Use connection pooling to manage and reuse database connections efficiently.

```python
# In settings.py
DATABASES = {
    'default': {
        'ENGINE': 'django.db.backends.postgresql',
        'NAME': 'mydatabase',
        'USER': 'mydatabaseuser',
        'PASSWORD': 'mypassword',
        'HOST': 'localhost',
        'PORT': '5432',
```

```
    'CONN_MAX_AGE': 600,  # Connection timeout (seconds)
}
```

b. Database Caching:

Utilize database caching for frequently accessed data to improve performance.

5. Logging Configuration:

Configure logging to capture and store application logs for monitoring and troubleshooting.

```python
# In settings.py
LOGGING = {
    'version': 1,
    'disable_existing_loggers': False,
    'handlers': {
        'file': {
            'level': 'INFO',
            'class': 'logging.FileHandler',
            'filename': '/path/to/your/logfile.log',
        },
    'loggers': {
        'django': {
```

```
            'handlers': ['file'],
            'level': 'INFO',
            'propagate': True,
```

6. Deployment Tools:

Choose deployment tools or platforms suited for deploying Django applications.

a. Docker:

Containerize your Django application using Docker for consistency and portability.

```dockerfile
# Dockerfile
FROM python:3.8
ENV PYTHONUNBUFFERED 1
WORKDIR /code
COPY requirements.txt /code/
RUN pip install -r requirements.txt
COPY . /code/
```

b. Deployment Platforms:

Consider platforms like Heroku, AWS Elastic Beanstalk, or Google App Engine for easy deployment and scaling.

Configuring your Django application for deployment involves optimizing settings, implementing security measures, handling static files efficiently, configuring the database, setting up logging, and choosing appropriate deployment tools or platforms. By following best practices and considering factors such as scalability, security, and ease of management, you can ensure that your Django RESTful API is deployed successfully and runs smoothly in a production environment. Regular testing, monitoring, and maintenance are essential to keep your application secure, reliable, and performant over time.

Setting Up Continuous Integration and Continuous Delivery (CI/CD) for Efficient Updates

Setting up Continuous Integration and Continuous Delivery (CI/CD) for your Django RESTful API is crucial for streamlining the development process, automating testing, and ensuring efficient updates to your application. CI/CD pipelines automate the building, testing, and deployment of your code, reducing manual errors and enabling faster release cycles. Let's explore how to set up CI/CD for a Django API, including code examples and best practices.

1. **Choose a CI/CD Service:**

Several CI/CD services are available, such as GitHub Actions, GitLab CI/CD, CircleCI, and Jenkins. Choose a service that integrates well with your version control system and provides the features you need for your CI/CD workflow.

2. **Configure CI/CD Pipeline:**

a. Define Workflow:

Create a CI/CD workflow file in your project repository to define the steps for building, testing, and deploying your Django API.

```yaml
# .github/workflows/ci-cd.yml (for GitHub Actions)
name: CI/CD Pipeline

on:
  push:
    branches:
      - main

jobs:
  build:
    runs-on: ubuntu-latest
```

```
   steps:
     - name: Checkout code
       uses: actions/checkout@v2

     - name: Set up Python
       uses: actions/setup-python@v2
       with:
         python-version: '3.x'

     - name: Install dependencies
       run: pip install -r requirements.txt

     - name: Run tests
       run: pytest
```

b. Add Deployment Steps:

Extend the workflow to include deployment steps for deploying your Django API to your hosting platform.

```yaml
# .github/workflows/ci-cd.yml (continued)
     - name: Deploy to production
       uses: easingthemes/deploy-to-ssh@v2
       with:
         server_ip: ${{ secrets.SERVER_IP }}
```

```
          server_username: ${{
secrets.SERVER_USERNAME }}
          server_password: ${{
secrets.SERVER_PASSWORD }}
        script: |
          cd /path/to/your/django/project
          git pull origin main
          python manage.py migrate
          systemctl restart gunicorn
  ```

3. Set up Secrets:

Store sensitive information such as server credentials securely as secrets in your CI/CD service. Never expose sensitive information directly in your code or CI/CD configuration files.

4. Implement Automated Testing:

Ensure that your CI/CD pipeline includes automated tests to validate the functionality and integrity of your Django API.

a. Unit Tests:

Write unit tests for individual components of your Django API to verify their behavior.

```python
# Example unit test for views
from django.test import TestCase
from django.urls import reverse

class MyAPITestCase(TestCase):
    def test_my_api_endpoint(self):
        url = reverse('my-api-endpoint')
        response = self.client.get(url)
        self.assertEqual(response.status_code, 200)
```

b. Integration Tests:

Write integration tests to verify interactions between different components of your Django API.

```python
# Example integration test using Django REST framework's APIClient
from rest_framework.test import APITestCase

class MyAPIIntegrationTestCase(APITestCase):
    def test_my_api_endpoint(self):
        url = '/my-api-endpoint/'
        response = self.client.get(url)
        self.assertEqual(response.status_code, 200)
```

```

## 5. Configure Deployment:

Set up deployment scripts or configuration files to automate the deployment of your Django API to your hosting platform.

### a. Deployment Script:

Write a deployment script to handle tasks such as pulling the latest code from your repository, applying database migrations, and restarting the server.

```bash
#!/bin/bash

cd /path/to/your/django/project
git pull origin main
python manage.py migrate
systemctl restart gunicorn
```

b. Deployment Configuration:

Configure your hosting platform (e.g., AWS, Heroku, DigitalOcean) to automatically deploy your Django API using the deployment script.
```

6. Monitor and Review:

Regularly monitor your CI/CD pipeline and review its performance to identify areas for improvement and optimization.

a. Monitor Build Status:

Monitor the build status of your CI/CD pipeline to ensure that builds are passing successfully and deployments are occurring as expected.

b. Review Test Results:

Review the results of automated tests to identify any failures or regressions and take corrective actions as needed.

7. Rollback Strategy:

Implement a rollback strategy in your CI/CD pipeline to revert to a previous version of your Django API in case of deployment failures or unexpected issues.

a. Automated Rollback:

Configure your CI/CD pipeline to automatically trigger a rollback if deployment fails or if automated tests detect regressions.

b. Manual Rollback:

Provide a manual rollback option to developers or operations teams to manually trigger a rollback if necessary.

8. Environment Management:

Utilize environment management tools to manage different environments (e.g., development, staging, production) and ensure consistency across deployments.

a. Environment Variables:

Use environment variables to configure settings that vary between environments, such as database credentials and API keys.

b. Infrastructure as Code (IaC):

Use infrastructure as code tools like Terraform or AWS CloudFormation to provision and manage infrastructure resources consistently across environments.

9. Scalability and Performance Testing:

Include scalability and performance testing in your CI/CD pipeline to ensure that your Django API can handle increasing loads and maintain optimal performance.

a. Load Testing:

Conduct load tests to simulate high traffic volumes and identify performance bottlenecks in your Django API.

b. Scalability Testing:

Test the scalability of your Django API by gradually increasing the load and measuring the response times and resource utilization.

10. Security Testing:

Integrate security testing into your CI/CD pipeline to identify and mitigate security vulnerabilities in your Django API.

a. Static Code Analysis:

Use static code analysis tools to identify security vulnerabilities, code smells, and best practice violations in your Django codebase.

b. Dependency Scanning:

Scan dependencies for known vulnerabilities and ensure that all dependencies are up to date and patched against security vulnerabilities.

11. Compliance and Governance:

Ensure compliance with regulatory requirements and governance policies by incorporating compliance checks into your CI/CD pipeline.

a. Compliance Checks:

Automate compliance checks to ensure that your Django API meets regulatory requirements such as GDPR, HIPAA, or PCI DSS.

b. Governance Policies:

Enforce governance policies related to code quality, security, and access controls through automated checks in your CI/CD pipeline.

Setting up a robust CI/CD pipeline for your Django RESTful API involves implementing automated rollback strategies, managing environments effectively, conducting scalability and performance testing, integrating security testing, and ensuring compliance with regulatory requirements and governance policies. By incorporating these practices into your CI/CD pipeline, you can accelerate the delivery of updates to your Django API while ensuring reliability, security, and compliance. Continuous monitoring, review, and optimization of your CI/CD pipeline are essential to maintaining its effectiveness and ensuring the successful and efficient delivery of updates to your Django API.

Chapter 13

Django REST Framework: Building RESTful APIs with Streamlined Functionality

Django REST Framework (DRF) is a powerful toolkit for building Web APIs in Django, providing a set of tools and libraries to simplify the creation of RESTful APIs. With DRF, you can quickly build APIs with features such as serialization, authentication, permissions, and viewsets, making it easier to develop robust and scalable APIs. Let's explore how to use Django REST Framework to build RESTful APIs with streamlined functionality, including code examples and best practices.

1. Installation:

To get started with Django REST Framework, you first need to install it into your Django project. You can install DRF using pip:

```bash
pip install djangorestframework
```

2. Setting up Django REST Framework:

After installing DRF, you need to configure it in your Django project's settings.py file:

```python
# settings.py
INSTALLED_APPS = [
    ...
    'rest_framework',
```

3. Serializers:

Serializers in DRF convert complex data types such as querysets and model instances to native Python data types that can be easily rendered into JSON, XML, or other content types. Let's create a simple serializer for a Django model:

```python
# serializers.py
from rest_framework import serializers
from .models import MyModel

class MyModelSerializer(serializers.ModelSerializer):
    class Meta:
        model = MyModel
        fields = '__all__'
```

4. Views:

Views in DRF define the logic for handling HTTP requests and generating responses. You can create views using function-based views or class-based views. Here's an example of a function-based view:

```python
# views.py
from rest_framework.decorators import api_view
from rest_framework.response import Response

@api_view(['GET'])
def my_view(request):
    data = {'message': 'Hello, world!'}
    return Response(data)
```

And here's an example of a class-based view using DRF's generic views:

```python
# views.py
from rest_framework.views import APIView
from rest_framework.response import Response
from .models import MyModel
from .serializers import MyModelSerializer
```

```python
class MyModelAPIView(APIView):
    def get(self, request):
        queryset = MyModel.objects.all()
        serializer = MyModelSerializer(queryset, many=True)
        return Response(serializer.data)
```

5. URLs:

You need to define URL patterns to route HTTP requests to the appropriate views in your Django project's urls.py file:

```python
# urls.py
from django.urls import path
from . import views

urlpatterns = [
    path('my-api/', views.my_view),
    path('my-model-api/', views.MyModelAPIView.as_view()),
]
```

6. Authentication and Permissions:

DRF provides built-in support for authentication and permissions, allowing you to secure your APIs easily. You can configure authentication classes and permission classes in your views or settings:

```python
# settings.py
REST_FRAMEWORK = {
    'DEFAULT_AUTHENTICATION_CLASSES': [
        'rest_framework.authentication.BasicAuthentication',
        'rest_framework.authentication.SessionAuthentication',
    ],
    'DEFAULT_PERMISSION_CLASSES': [
        'rest_framework.permissions.IsAuthenticated',
```

7. Viewsets and Routers:

Viewsets in DRF provide a way to organize related views into a single class, simplifying the structure of your API views. You can use routers to automatically generate URL patterns for viewsets:

```python
# views.py
```

```python
from rest_framework import viewsets
from .models import MyModel
from .serializers import MyModelSerializer

class MyModelViewSet(viewsets.ModelViewSet):
    queryset = MyModel.objects.all()
    serializer_class = MyModelSerializer
```

```python
# urls.py
from rest_framework.routers import DefaultRouter
from .views import MyModelViewSet

router = DefaultRouter()
router.register(r'my-model', MyModelViewSet)

urlpatterns = router.urls
```

8. Pagination and Filtering:

DRF provides built-in support for pagination and filtering, allowing you to control the size of response data and filter querysets based on query parameters:

```python
# settings.py
```

```
REST_FRAMEWORK = {
    'DEFAULT_PAGINATION_CLASS':
'rest_framework.pagination.PageNumberPagination',
    'PAGE_SIZE': 10
}
```

```python
# views.py
from rest_framework import generics
from .models import MyModel
from .serializers import MyModelSerializer
from rest_framework.filters import SearchFilter

class MyModelList(generics.ListAPIView):
    queryset = MyModel.objects.all()
    serializer_class = MyModelSerializer
    filter_backends = [SearchFilter]
    search_fields = ['name', 'description']
```

projects. Additionally, DRF offers extensibility and flexibility, allowing you to customize and extend its functionality according to your project's specific requirements. Here are some additional features and best practices to consider when building RESTful APIs with Django REST Framework:

9. Content Negotiation:

DRF supports content negotiation, allowing your API to respond with different content types (e.g., JSON, XML) based on the client's Accept header. You can configure content negotiation settings in your project's settings.py file:

```python
# settings.py
REST_FRAMEWORK = {
    'DEFAULT_RENDERER_CLASSES': [
        'rest_framework.renderers.JSONRenderer',
        'rest_framework.renderers.XMLRenderer',
}
```

10. Versioning:

Consider implementing API versioning to manage changes to your API's functionality over time. DRF provides built-in support for versioning, allowing you to version your API by URL, header, or query parameter.

```python
# urls.py
from rest_framework.urlpatterns import format_suffix_patterns
```

```python
from . import views

urlpatterns = [
    path('my-api/v1/', views.my_view),

urlpatterns = format_suffix_patterns(urlpatterns)
```

11. Throttling:

Throttling allows you to limit the number of requests a user can make to your API within a certain time period, preventing abuse and ensuring fair usage of resources. DRF provides built-in support for throttling, allowing you to configure throttling policies based on user or IP address.

```python
# settings.py
REST_FRAMEWORK = {
    'DEFAULT_THROTTLE_CLASSES': [
        'rest_framework.throttling.AnonRateThrottle',
        'rest_framework.throttling.UserRateThrottle',
    ],
    'DEFAULT_THROTTLE_RATES': {
        'anon': '10/day',
        'user': '1000/day',
    }
```

```

## 12. HATEOAS:

Hypermedia as the Engine of Application State (HATEOAS) is a principle of RESTful APIs that provides links within API responses to navigate to related resources. While DRF does not provide built-in support for HATEOAS, you can implement it manually by including links in your API responses.

```python
# views.py
from rest_framework.response import Response
from rest_framework.decorators import api_view
from django.urls import reverse

@api_view(['GET'])
def my_view(request):
    data = {
        'message': 'Hello, world!',
        'links': {
            'self': reverse('my-view'),
            'other_resource': reverse('other-resource'),
        }
    }
    return Response(data)
```
```

Django REST Framework is a versatile and feature-rich toolkit for building RESTful APIs in Django. By leveraging its powerful features such as serializers, views, authentication, permissions, viewsets, pagination, filtering, content negotiation, versioning, throttling, and HATEOAS, you can develop efficient and scalable APIs with streamlined functionality. Additionally, DRF's extensibility and flexibility allow you to customize and extend its functionality to meet the specific requirements of your projects. Whether you're building a simple API or a complex web application, Django REST Framework provides the tools you need to develop robust and maintainable APIs in Django.

Integrating with Other Systems: Utilizing Django APIs in Different Applications

Integrating Django APIs with other systems is a common scenario in modern software development, allowing different applications to communicate and share data seamlessly. Whether it's integrating with frontend web applications, mobile apps, external services, or IoT devices, Django APIs provide a flexible and robust solution for building interconnected systems. In this guide, we'll explore how to integrate Django APIs with different applications, along with code examples and best practices.

1. Integrating with Frontend Web Applications:

Frontend web applications often consume data from Django APIs to display dynamic content to users. You can integrate Django APIs with frontend frameworks like React, Angular, or Vue.js using AJAX requests or dedicated libraries like Axios.

a. Fetching Data from Django API:

```javascript
// Example using Axios to fetch data from Django API in a React component
import React, { useState, useEffect } from 'react';
import axios from 'axios';

const MyComponent = () => {
  const [data, setData] = useState([]);

  useEffect(() => {
    axios.get('https://example.com/api/data/')
      .then(response => {
        setData(response.data);
      })
      .catch(error => {
        console.error('Error fetching data:', error);
  []);
  return (
    <div>
```

```
      {data.map(item => (
         <div key={item.id}>{item.name}</div>
      ))}
   </div>
```

b. Handling CORS:

Ensure that your Django API allows Cross-Origin Resource Sharing (CORS) to allow requests from frontend applications hosted on different domains.

```python
# settings.py
CORS_ALLOW_ALL_ORIGINS = True
```

2. Integrating with Mobile Apps:

Mobile apps can communicate with Django APIs to access backend services and retrieve data. You can use libraries like Retrofit (for Android) or Alamofire (for iOS) to make HTTP requests to Django APIs.

a. Making HTTP Requests:

```swift
```

```swift
// Example using Alamofire to make HTTP requests to Django API in Swift (iOS)
import Alamofire

AF.request("https://example.com/api/data/")
    .validate()
    .responseDecodable(of: [Item].self) { response in
        guard let items = response.value else {
            print("Error: \(response.error)")
            return
        }
        print("Items: \(items)")
```

3. Integrating with External Services:

Django APIs can integrate with external services, such as payment gateways, email services, or third-party APIs, to extend functionality or access additional features.

a. Sending Emails:

```python
# Example using Django's built-in email functionality to send emails via Django API
from django.core.mail import send_mail
```

```
send_mail(
    'Subject here',
    'Here is the message.',
    'from@example.com',
    ['to@example.com'],
    fail_silently=False,
)
```

b. Consuming Third-Party APIs:

```python
# Example using requests library to consume a third-party API in Django view
import requests

def my_view(request):
    response = requests.get('https://api.example.com/data/')
    data = response.json()
    return JsonResponse(data)
```

4. Integrating with IoT Devices:

Django APIs can communicate with IoT devices to send commands, receive sensor data, or control actuators. You can use Django's built-in views or Django Channels for real-time communication with IoT devices.

a. Receiving Sensor Data:

```python
# Example using Django Channels to receive sensor data from IoT devices in real-time
from channels.generic.websocket import WebsocketConsumer
import json

class SensorConsumer(WebsocketConsumer):
    def connect(self):
        self.accept()

    def disconnect(self, close_code):
        pass

    def receive(self, text_data):
        data = json.loads(text_data)
        # Process sensor data
```

5. Authentication and Authorization:

Ensure that your Django API implements proper authentication and authorization mechanisms to secure access to sensitive resources and endpoints.

a. Token Authentication:

```python
# settings.py
REST_FRAMEWORK = {
    'DEFAULT_AUTHENTICATION_CLASSES': [
        'rest_framework.authentication.TokenAuthentication',
    ],
    'DEFAULT_PERMISSION_CLASSES': [
        'rest_framework.permissions.IsAuthenticated',
    ]
}
```

b. OAuth2 Authentication:

```python
# settings.py
INSTALLED_APPS = [
    ...
    'oauth2_provider',

OAUTH2_PROVIDER = {
```

```
    'SCOPES': {'read': 'Read scope', 'write': 'Write scope',
'groups': 'Access to your groups'},
    'ACCESS_TOKEN_EXPIRE_SECONDS': 3600,
}
```

6. Data Serialization and Validation:

When integrating Django APIs with different applications, it's essential to ensure proper data serialization and validation to maintain data integrity and consistency across systems.

a. Serialization:

Serialize data returned by Django APIs into a format suitable for consumption by the client application. Use Django REST Framework's serializers to serialize Django model instances or custom data structures into JSON, XML, or other formats.

```python
# serializers.py
from rest_framework import serializers
from .models import MyModel

class MyModelSerializer(serializers.ModelSerializer):
    class Meta:
```

```
        model = MyModel
        fields = '__all__'
```

b. Validation:

Validate data received by Django APIs from client applications to ensure that it meets the required format and constraints. Use serializers' validation features to validate input data before processing it.

```python
# serializers.py
from rest_framework import serializers

class MySerializer(serializers.Serializer):
    name = serializers.CharField(max_length=100)
    email = serializers.EmailField()

    def validate_name(self, value):
        # Custom validation logic for 'name' field
        if not value.isalpha():
            raise serializers.ValidationError("Name must contain only alphabetic characters")
        return value
```

7. Error Handling:

Implement proper error handling mechanisms in your Django APIs to provide meaningful error responses to client applications in case of errors or exceptions.

a. Custom Exception Handling:

Define custom exception handlers to catch and handle specific types of exceptions and return appropriate error responses.

```python
# views.py
from rest_framework.views import exception_handler
from rest_framework.response import Response
from rest_framework import status

def custom_exception_handler(exc, context):
    response = exception_handler(exc, context)

    if response is not None:
        response.data['status_code'] = response.status_code

    return response

# settings.py
REST_FRAMEWORK = {
```

```
    'EXCEPTION_HANDLER':
'myapp.views.custom_exception_handler'
}
```

8. Rate Limiting:

Implement rate limiting in your Django APIs to prevent abuse and ensure fair usage of resources. Rate limiting restricts the number of requests a client can make within a certain time period.

a. Throttling:

Use Django REST Framework's throttling feature to implement rate limiting based on the number of requests per user or IP address.

```python
# settings.py
REST_FRAMEWORK = {
    'DEFAULT_THROTTLE_CLASSES': [
        'rest_framework.throttling.AnonRateThrottle',
        'rest_framework.throttling.UserRateThrottle',
    ],
    'DEFAULT_THROTTLE_RATES': {
        'anon': '100/day',
        'user': '1000/day',
```

}
```

## 9. Monitoring and Logging:

Monitor your Django APIs for performance metrics, errors, and other relevant data to identify issues and optimize performance.

### a. Logging:

Use Django's built-in logging framework to log important events and information about requests, responses, and errors.

```python
# settings.py
LOGGING = {
    'version': 1,
    'disable_existing_loggers': False,
    'handlers': {
        'file': {
            'level': 'DEBUG',
            'class': 'logging.FileHandler',
            'filename': '/path/to/logfile.log',
        },
    },
    'loggers': {
        'django': {

```
            'handlers': ['file'],
            'level': 'DEBUG',
            'propagate': True,
    },
```

b. Performance Monitoring:

Use tools like Django Debug Toolbar, New Relic, or Datadog to monitor performance metrics such as response times, request throughput, and database queries.

Integrating Django APIs with different applications requires careful consideration of data serialization, validation, error handling, rate limiting, and monitoring. By following best practices and implementing these features, you can ensure that your Django APIs are robust, secure, and performant in diverse integration scenarios. Additionally, regular monitoring and optimization of your Django APIs are essential to maintain reliability and scalability as your application evolves and grows. With proper integration practices in place, you can build interoperable and scalable systems that meet the needs of your users and stakeholders.

Building Scalable and Secure API Ecosystems

Building scalable and secure API ecosystems is crucial for modern software development, enabling organizations to deliver reliable, efficient, and interoperable services to users and stakeholders. In this guide, we'll explore best practices and techniques for building scalable and secure API ecosystems using Django, focusing on scalability, security, authentication, authorization, monitoring, and governance.

1. Scalability:

Scalability is essential for handling increasing loads and ensuring consistent performance as your API ecosystem grows. Here's how you can build scalable API ecosystems with Django:

a. Horizontal Scaling:

Use load balancers and distributed architectures to horizontally scale your Django APIs across multiple servers or containers. Tools like Docker Swarm or Kubernetes can help manage containerized Django applications for horizontal scalability.

```python
# settings.py
```

```
ALLOWED_HOSTS = ['*']  # Allow all hosts for horizontal scaling
```

b. Asynchronous Processing:

Leverage asynchronous processing with libraries like Celery and Redis to offload long-running tasks from your Django API server and improve responsiveness.

```python
# tasks.py
from celery import Celery

app = Celery('tasks', broker='redis://localhost:6379/0')

@app.task
def process_data(data):
    # Long-running task
    pass
```

2. Security:

Security is paramount in API ecosystems to protect sensitive data, prevent unauthorized access, and mitigate security threats. Here's how you can build secure API ecosystems with Django:

a. Authentication:

Implement robust authentication mechanisms such as token-based authentication or OAuth2 to verify the identity of clients accessing your APIs.

```python
# settings.py
REST_FRAMEWORK = {
    'DEFAULT_AUTHENTICATION_CLASSES': [

'rest_framework.authentication.TokenAuthentication',

'rest_framework.authentication.SessionAuthentication',
}
```

b. Authorization:

Enforce fine-grained access control with Django REST Framework's permission classes to restrict access to resources based on user roles and permissions.

```python
# views.py
from rest_framework.permissions import IsAuthenticated
```

```
class MyAPIView(APIView):
    permission_classes = [IsAuthenticated]
```

3. Rate Limiting:

Implement rate limiting to prevent abuse and ensure fair usage of your API resources. Throttling allows you to restrict the number of requests clients can make within a certain time frame.

```python
# settings.py
REST_FRAMEWORK = {
    'DEFAULT_THROTTLE_CLASSES': [
        'rest_framework.throttling.AnonRateThrottle',
        'rest_framework.throttling.UserRateThrottle',
    ],
    'DEFAULT_THROTTLE_RATES': {
        'anon': '100/day',
        'user': '1000/day',
    }
}
```

4. Monitoring:

Monitoring your API ecosystem is essential for detecting and addressing performance issues, security vulnerabilities, and other operational concerns. Here's how you can monitor your Django API ecosystem:

a. Logging:

Use Django's built-in logging framework to log important events, errors, and debugging information. Configure logging to store logs centrally for easy analysis.

```python
# settings.py
LOGGING = {
  'version': 1,
  'disable_existing_loggers': False,
  'handlers': {
    'file': {
      'level': 'DEBUG',
      'class': 'logging.FileHandler',
      'filename': '/path/to/logfile.log',
    },
  },
  'loggers': {
    'django': {
      'handlers': ['file'],
      'level': 'DEBUG',
      'propagate': True,
```

    },
```

### b. Performance Monitoring:

Use monitoring tools like Prometheus, Grafana, or Datadog to track performance metrics such as response times, error rates, and throughput.

## 5. Governance:

Establish governance policies and procedures to ensure compliance, manage risks, and maintain the quality of your API ecosystem. Here are some governance practices to consider:

### a. Compliance:

Ensure compliance with regulatory requirements such as GDPR, HIPAA, or PCI DSS by implementing appropriate data protection measures and privacy controls.

### b. API Documentation:

Provide comprehensive documentation for your APIs, including usage guidelines, examples, and reference
```

documentation, to facilitate integration and usage by developers.

c. Versioning:

Implement versioning for your APIs to manage changes and updates without breaking backward compatibility. Use semantic versioning to communicate changes effectively.

```python
# urls.py
from rest_framework.urlpatterns import format_suffix_patterns
from . import views

urlpatterns = [
    path('my-api/v1/', views.my_view),
]

urlpatterns = format_suffix_patterns(urlpatterns)
```

Building scalable and secure API ecosystems with Django requires a combination of technical expertise, best practices, and governance principles. By following the guidelines outlined above, you can design and implement API ecosystems that meet the needs of your organization and stakeholders while ensuring scalability, security, monitoring, and governance. With a robust API ecosystem in place, you can deliver reliable, efficient, and interoperable services that drive innovation and create value for your users and customers.

Conclusion

In conclusion, RESTful API development with Django offers a powerful and flexible solution for building robust and scalable APIs that drive modern software ecosystems. Throughout this guide, we've explored various aspects of Django API development, including optimization for scalability, implementation of security measures, integration with different applications, and establishment of governance practices.

By leveraging Django's extensive features and the Django REST Framework toolkit, developers can streamline the process of building APIs while ensuring high performance, security, and maintainability. From serializing data to handling authentication and authorization, Django provides the tools necessary to create APIs that meet the diverse needs of today's digital landscape.

Furthermore, integrating Django APIs with frontend web applications, mobile apps, external services, and IoT devices allows organizations to create interconnected systems that deliver seamless user experiences. Whether it's fetching data from a database, processing requests asynchronously, or interacting with third-party APIs,

Django APIs offer the flexibility and extensibility needed to support a wide range of use cases.

In addition to technical considerations, governance practices such as compliance, documentation, and versioning play a crucial role in the success of API ecosystems. By adhering to best practices and implementing governance frameworks, organizations can ensure that their APIs are secure, well-documented, and easy to manage, fostering collaboration and innovation among developers.

In today's digital age, where connectivity and interoperability are key drivers of success, Django APIs serve as the backbone of modern software ecosystems. With their ability to scale, secure, and integrate seamlessly with other systems, Django APIs empower organizations to innovate, adapt, and thrive in an ever-evolving technological landscape. Whether you're building a simple RESTful API or a complex ecosystem of interconnected services, Django provides the tools and frameworks necessary to turn your ideas into reality.

Appendix

Common Django Libraries and Tools for API Development

Developing RESTful APIs with Django is greatly enhanced by the extensive ecosystem of libraries and tools available. These libraries and tools provide developers with ready-made solutions for common tasks such as serialization, authentication, documentation, testing, and more. In this guide, we'll explore some of the most commonly used Django libraries and tools for API development, along with code examples and best practices.

1. Django REST Framework (DRF):

Django REST Framework is the go-to toolkit for building Web APIs in Django. It provides powerful features for serialization, authentication, permissions, viewsets, routers, pagination, filtering, and more, making it easier to develop robust and scalable APIs.

```bash
pip install djangorestframework
```

2. Django REST Swagger:

Django REST Swagger generates interactive API documentation for your Django REST Framework APIs.

It automatically generates a UI based on your API schema, allowing developers to explore endpoints, make requests, and view responses directly from the browser.

```bash
pip install django-rest-swagger
```

3. Django OAuth Toolkit:

Django OAuth Toolkit provides OAuth2 support for Django applications, allowing you to implement OAuth2 authentication flows for securing your APIs. It supports both token and authorization code grant types out of the box.

```bash
pip install django-oauth-toolkit
```

4. Django Filter:

Django Filter provides a simple way to filter querysets dynamically based on request parameters. It's especially useful for building APIs with filtering capabilities, allowing clients to retrieve only the data they need.

```bash
pip install django-filter
```

```

**5. Django Cors Headers:**

Django Cors Headers adds Cross-Origin Resource Sharing (CORS) headers to Django responses, allowing you to control access to your APIs from web browsers. It's essential for allowing requests from frontend applications hosted on different domains.

```bash

pip install django-cors-headers

```

6. Django Simple JWT:

Django Simple JWT provides JSON Web Token (JWT) authentication for Django REST Framework APIs. It's a lightweight and easy-to-use library for implementing token-based authentication in your Django applications.

```bash

pip install djangorestframework-simplejwt

```

7. Django Test Plus:

Django Test Plus extends Django's built-in testing framework with additional utilities and helpers for testing APIs. It provides shortcuts for creating test
```

objects, making requests, and asserting responses, making it easier to write comprehensive test suites for your APIs.

```bash

pip install django-test-plus

```

8. Django Debug Toolbar:

Django Debug Toolbar adds a configurable toolbar to the bottom of the browser window for debugging Django applications. It provides insights into request/response cycles, database queries, template rendering, and more, helping developers diagnose and fix issues quickly.

```bash

pip install django-debug-toolbar

```

9. Django Cors Middleware:

Django Cors Middleware is another option for adding CORS headers to Django responses. It's a simple middleware that intercepts responses and adds the necessary CORS headers based on configured settings.

```bash

pip install django-cors-middleware
```

```

## 10. Django Guardian:

Django Guardian provides object-level permissions for Django applications, allowing you to assign permissions to specific objects rather than entire models. It integrates seamlessly with Django's authentication and authorization system, providing fine-grained access control for your APIs.

```bash

pip install django-guardian

```

11. Django Rest Auth:

Django Rest Auth is an extension of Django REST Framework that provides authentication endpoints for handling user registration, login, logout, password reset, and other authentication-related tasks. It integrates seamlessly with Django's authentication system and provides customizable views and serializers for authentication flows.

```bash

pip install django-rest-auth

```

12. Django Rest Framework Permissions:
```

Django REST Framework Permissions provides a set of built-in permission classes for controlling access to API views based on user permissions and roles. It allows you to restrict access to certain endpoints based on predefined rules, ensuring that only authorized users can perform specific actions.

```python
# views.py

from rest_framework.permissions import IsAuthenticated

class MyAPIView(APIView):
    permission_classes = [IsAuthenticated]
```

13. Django Rest Framework Simple JWT:

Django REST Framework Simple JWT is a library for adding JSON Web Token (JWT) authentication to Django REST Framework APIs. It provides simple and secure token-based authentication, allowing clients to authenticate with your API using JWT tokens.

```python
# settings.py

REST_FRAMEWORK = {
```

```
'DEFAULT_AUTHENTICATION_CLASSES': [

'rest_framework_simplejwt.authentication.JWTAuthentication',

}
```

14. Django Rest Framework Serializer Extensions:

Django REST Framework Serializer Extensions extends DRF's serialization capabilities with additional features such as custom fields, nested serializers, read-only fields, and more. It allows you to customize how data is serialized and deserialized in your API views.

```bash
pip install djangorestframework-serializer-extensions
```

15. Django Rest Framework GIS:

Django REST Framework GIS provides geographic information system (GIS) support for Django REST Framework, allowing you to build APIs for working with spatial data. It adds support for serializing and deserializing GIS data types such as Point, LineString, Polygon, and GeometryCollection.

```bash
```

pip install djangorestframework-gis

```

## 16. Django Rest Framework Bulk:

Django REST Framework Bulk adds support for bulk operations (create, update, delete) to Django REST Framework APIs. It allows clients to send multiple requests in a single HTTP request, reducing latency and improving performance for bulk operations.

```bash
pip install djangorestframework-bulk

```

17. Django Rest Framework JWT Blacklist:

Django REST Framework JWT Blacklist adds support for token blacklisting to Django REST Framework Simple JWT. It allows you to revoke JWT tokens and prevent them from being used after they have been invalidated.

```bash
pip install djangorestframework-jwt-blacklist

```

18. Django Rest Framework JSON API:
```

Django REST Framework JSON API provides support for the JSON API specification, allowing you to build APIs that adhere to the JSON API standard. It includes serializers, views, and pagination classes for working with JSON API data structures.

```bash
pip install djangorestframework-jsonapi
```

These Django libraries and tools provide essential functionality for building robust, scalable, and secure RESTful APIs. By leveraging these libraries and tools, developers can accelerate the development process, improve code quality, and enhance the overall user experience of their APIs. Whether you're building a simple CRUD API or a complex API ecosystem, these libraries and tools offer the features and flexibility you need to succeed in your API development projects. Experiment with different libraries and tools to find the ones that best fit your project's requirements and workflow, and continue to explore the vibrant Django ecosystem for new and innovative solutions.

Troubleshooting Tips and Error Handling in Django APIs

Troubleshooting and error handling are essential aspects of developing RESTful APIs with Django. As developers, encountering errors and debugging issues is inevitable, but having effective strategies for troubleshooting can greatly streamline the development process and improve the quality of your APIs. In this guide, we'll explore some common troubleshooting tips and error handling techniques in Django APIs, along with code examples and best practices.

1. Enable Debugging:

Django provides a built-in debugging tool that helps developers identify and fix errors quickly. Ensure that debugging is enabled in your Django settings during development:

```python
# settings.py
DEBUG = True
```

With debugging enabled, Django will display detailed error pages with stack traces, making it easier to pinpoint the source of the issue.

2. Logging:

Logging is a crucial tool for troubleshooting and error handling in Django APIs. Use Django's built-in logging framework to log important events, errors, and debugging information to a file or console:

```python
# settings.py
LOGGING = {
  'version': 1,
  'disable_existing_loggers': False,
  'handlers': {
    'file': {
      'level': 'DEBUG',
      'class': 'logging.FileHandler',
      'filename': '/path/to/logfile.log',
    },
  'loggers': {
    'django': {
      'handlers': ['file'],
      'level': 'DEBUG',
      'propagate': True,
  },
```

3. Custom Error Pages:

Customize error pages to provide users with helpful information when they encounter errors. You can define custom error views in your Django application to render custom error pages:

```python
# views.py
from django.shortcuts import render

def handler404(request, exception):
    return render(request, '404.html', status=404)

def handler500(request):
    return render(request, '500.html', status=500)
```

4. Exception Handling:

Handle exceptions gracefully in your Django API views to prevent crashes and provide meaningful error messages to clients. Use try-except blocks to catch exceptions and handle them appropriately:

```python
# views.py
from rest_framework.views import APIView
from rest_framework.response import Response
from rest_framework import status

class MyView(APIView):
    def get(self, request):
        try:
```

```
    # Code that may raise an exception
    data = ...
    return Response(data)
except Exception as e:
    return Response({'error': str(e)}, status=status.HTTP_500_INTERNAL_SERVER_ERROR)
```

5. Django Debug Toolbar:

Django Debug Toolbar is a powerful debugging tool that provides insights into request/response cycles, database queries, template rendering, and more. Install and configure Django Debug Toolbar to diagnose performance issues and identify bottlenecks in your API:

```bash
pip install django-debug-toolbar
```

6. Error Reporting Services:

Consider using error reporting services like Sentry or Rollbar to track and monitor errors in your Django APIs. These services capture exceptions and provide detailed reports, helping you identify and fix issues proactively:

```bash
pip install sentry-sdk
```

7. Testing and Test Coverage:

Write comprehensive test suites for your Django APIs to catch errors and regressions early in the development process. Use tools like Django's TestCase and coverage.py to ensure adequate test coverage:

```python
# tests.py
from django.test import TestCase
from myapp.models import MyModel

class MyModelTestCase(TestCase):
    def test_something(self):
        # Test code here
        pass
```

8. API Documentation:

Provide clear and comprehensive documentation for your Django APIs to help developers understand how to use them correctly. Use tools like Django REST

Swagger or DRF's built-in documentation to generate interactive API documentation:

```bash
pip install django-rest-swagger
```

Troubleshooting and error handling are critical aspects of developing robust and reliable RESTful APIs with Django. By following the tips and techniques outlined in this guide, you can effectively identify, diagnose, and resolve issues in your Django APIs, ensuring a smooth and error-free user experience. Remember to enable debugging, use logging effectively, handle exceptions gracefully, leverage debugging tools, monitor errors with reporting services, write comprehensive tests, and provide clear documentation to facilitate troubleshooting and error handling in your Django API development process. With these strategies in place, you can build high-quality APIs that meet the needs of your users and stakeholders.

Glossary of terms

Here's a glossary of terms commonly used in RESTful API development with Django:

1. API (Application Programming Interface): A set of rules and protocols that allows different software applications to communicate and interact with each other.

2. REST (Representational State Transfer): An architectural style for designing networked applications, where resources are represented as unique URIs and can be manipulated using standard HTTP methods.

3. RESTful: Adhering to the principles of REST, including stateless communication, client-server architecture, uniform interface, and layered system.

4. Django: A high-level Python web framework that encourages rapid development and clean, pragmatic design. It provides built-in features for creating web applications, including APIs.

5. Django REST Framework (DRF): A powerful toolkit for building Web APIs in Django. It provides serializers, views, authentication, permissions, pagination, and more to streamline API development.

6. Serializer: A component of DRF that converts complex data types, such as Django model instances, into native Python data types that can be easily rendered into JSON, XML, or other content types.

7. View: In the context of Django APIs, a view is a Python function or class that receives web requests and returns web responses. Views are responsible for processing incoming requests and generating appropriate responses.

8. Endpoint: A specific URL in a web API that corresponds to a resource or a collection of resources. Clients can make requests to endpoints to interact with the API.

9. HTTP Methods: Standardized actions that can be performed on resources using HTTP protocol. Common HTTP methods include GET (retrieve data), POST (create data), PUT (update data), PATCH (partially update data), and DELETE (delete data).

10. URI (Uniform Resource Identifier): A string of characters used to identify a resource on the internet. In RESTful APIs, URIs are used to address resources and endpoints.

11. Authentication: The process of verifying the identity of a user or client accessing an API. Authentication mechanisms include token-based authentication, OAuth2, and basic authentication.

12. Authorization: The process of determining whether a user or client has permission to access a specific resource or perform a specific action within an API. Authorization mechanisms include role-based access control, permissions, and policies.

13. Middleware: A framework of hooks into Django's request/response processing. Middleware can modify requests, responses, or behavior at various stages of the request/response lifecycle.

14. Pagination: The process of splitting large sets of data into smaller pages to improve performance and reduce load on the server. Pagination allows clients to retrieve data in manageable chunks.

15. CORS (Cross-Origin Resource Sharing): A mechanism that allows web browsers to make cross-origin requests to APIs hosted on different domains. CORS headers control access to resources from different origins.

16. Throttling: Limiting the number of requests a client can make to an API within a specified time period. Throttling helps prevent abuse and ensures fair usage of API resources.

17. Serialization: The process of converting complex data types, such as Django model instances, into a format that can be easily transmitted over the network, such as JSON or XML.

18. Deserialization: The process of converting serialized data received from a client into native Python data types that can be processed and manipulated by the server.

19. Versioning: The practice of managing changes to an API's functionality over time by assigning version numbers to different releases. Versioning helps maintain backward compatibility and manage API evolution.

20. Middleware: A framework of hooks into Django's request/response processing. Middleware can modify requests, responses, or behavior at various stages of the request/response lifecycle.

This glossary provides a foundation for understanding the terminology and concepts used in RESTful API development with Django. Familiarizing yourself with these terms will help you navigate the world of Django APIs more effectively and communicate with other developers and stakeholders more confidently.

www.ingramcontent.com/pod-product-compliance
Lightning Source LLC
Chambersburg PA
CBHW031607210526
45464CB00004B/1468